THE PRIME
SOLUTION

CLOSE THE VALUE GAP, INCREASE MARGINS, AND WIN THE COMPLEX SALE

JEFF THULL

Dearborn™
Trade Publishing
A **Kaplan Professional** Company

This publication is designed to provide accurate and authoritative information in regard to the subject matter covered. It is sold with the understanding that the publisher is not engaged in rendering legal, accounting, or other professional service. If legal advice or other expert assistance is required, the services of a competent professional should be sought.

Vice President and Publisher: Cynthia A. Zigmund
Acquisitions Editor: Michael Cunningham
Senior Project Editor: Trey Thoelcke
Interior Design: Lucy Jenkins
Cover Design: Design Solutions
Typesetting: Elizabeth Pitts

Published by Dearborn Trade Publishing
A Kaplan Professional Company

Printed in the United States of America

12 13 20 19 18 17 16 15

Library of Congress Cataloging-in-Publication Data

Thull, Jeff, 1949–
  The prime solution : close the value gap, increase margins, and win the complex sale / Jeff Thull.
      p.   cm.
  Includes index.
  ISBN 0-7931-9522-5
  1. Industrial marketing. 2. Sales management. 3. Selling. 4. Customer relations. 5. Value.   I. Title.
    HF5415.1263.T49   2005
    658.8′1—dc22

                                                2004015641

PRAISE FOR *THE PRIME SOLUTION*

*"If you sell a complex product, in a crowded competitive
environment, to customers with increasing expectations—
read* The Prime Solution *and put its principles to work.
We have implemented many of Jeff Thull's ideas successfully
at Motive, where we believe that enabling value outcomes—
not just selling software—is the key to success."*

MIKE MAPLES
Chief Marketing Officer, Motive, Inc.

"The concepts of The Prime Solution *have enriched my
professional and personal life and has helped the organizations I
work(ed) for to grow significantly in revenue and profitability.
This book examines why companies cannot capture the full value
of their solutions—and what they can do about it! A must-read.*

ROB CASTIEN
President, Spark Holland BV

*"I have been a vociferous reader of business books for 32 years.
No other writer has had more of a positive impact
on my business than Jeff Thull."*

RALPH S. HEATH III
President, Ovation Marketing

*"Jeff Thull has cracked the code on uniting the entire organization
in a singular approach to ensure that value promised
becomes value achieved. Senior management must be the
agent of change; the success examples in this book
highlight the why and the how very clearly."*

JACQUES J. MARCOTTE
VP General Manager, BTG Americas, Inc.

*"An essential read for anyone wondering why their 'solutions'
approach may not be working as planned. In a global industry
that faces daily pressures to treat high value solutions like
commodities, we are now breaking free of the crowded field of
solution providers by adopting many of the ideas of* The Prime
Solution*—ideas that are focused on creating and delivering
value—value that is truly recognized by our customers.*

MICHAEL HEIL
Global Marketing Director
BOC Process Gas Solutions

"Like a great physician, Jeff Thull accurately diagnoses the symptoms and causes of the disconnect between value capability and value reality. His prescription comes with a rich blend of proven examples and a deep, intuitive understanding of the problems faced by many companies that have great value to offer but that cannot overcome all of the hype in the marketplace. As a provider of complex enterprise solutions, The Prime Solution *gave us an excellent roadmap to step above the clutter and raise the bar for our competition."*

BRUCE KANNRY
CEO, nVISIA

"Jeff Thull again provides remarkable clarity to a very complex issue—how to set your organization apart in an overcrowded world of complex value promises. This book will not only become the standard for creating, delivering, and capturing value, but will serve as a wake-up call to those who are wondering why our great approaches of the past have derailed."

JEFF BOLKE
Vice President Worldwide Sales, Motive, Inc.

"This is a masterpiece! Jeff Thull is a genius presenter of practical yet transformational ideas that can readily help you and your company in really big ways."

NIDO R. QUBEIN
Chairman, Great Harvest Bread Company
Founder, National Speakers Association Foundation

The Prime Solution *provides a thought-provoking roadmap. Its cross-functional process is a breath of fresh air that defines how companies can ensure success in today's brave new world of business.*

JEFFREY L. TIMMS
Vice President of Sales and Marketing, Americas
Siemens Logistics and Assembly Solutions, EA

The Prime Solution *is the perfect extension to* Mastering the Complex Sale. *Jeff Thull concisely defines and points out how you can bridge the value gap. As the complex sales process we all face continues to become more complicated, relying on the roadmap and tools in* The Prime Solution *will keep you focused on what is value from the customer's point of view. Managing that side of the equation will leverage your success."*

JIM KIRKPATRICK
Vice President—General Products Group
Terumo Medical Corporation

"An insightful yet unsettling view of those value gaps we create with our own customers, followed by concise strategies on how we can deliver on the value promises we make to our customers. Closing these gaps is a must for sustained business growth, especially when you're involved in a complex sales process."

TOM WIDA
President, Biacore, Inc.

"Jeff Thull elegantly addresses how companies that are feeling burdened by competitive and commoditization pressures can ultimately succeed. Tomorrow's successful companies will be those that fully comprehend the inescapable wisdom of The Prime Solution's *message. Get ready for some profound realizations and a precise path to very stable and profitable business relationships."*

DONNY HOLENDER
Vice President—Sales, Universal Computer Systems, Inc.

"Jeff Thull offers a practical and comprehensive process for assuring that all parts of your organization are orchestrated to create and deliver valued solutions from the beginning. The characteristics of Prime Solutions are particularly insightful, as we constantly strive to develop unique solutions for our customers."

MICHAEL JONES
President and CEO, (i)Structure

"What first appeals is the pragmatic, street-tested advice. The Prime Solution *gives you a roadmap and language that every customer-facing professional in your organization can use to identify, quantify, and deliver tangible value through business transformation."*

DON ADDINGTON
President and CEO, Seagull Software

Contents

We at Shell Global Solutions were introduced to Jeff Thull through his first book, *Mastering the Complex Sale*. As I finished reading *The Prime Solution,* my first thought was that Jeff also wrote this book with Shell Global Solutions in mind. Providing solutions is a challenge in any business and it is particularly complex in our environment, the energy industry markets. Looking into the background of our organization should make it clear why we found Jeff's argument so compelling.

At Shell Global Solutions, our corporate heritage is unusual, if not unique. We originated as the research and technical service group within Royal Dutch Shell Group. Our sole charter was supporting Shell's business activities worldwide. As an internal service provider, we lived with our customers and were quite sensitive to our charter of uncovering value creation opportunities within Shell and delivering on our value promises.

By 1997, as cost pressures began to threaten the viability of such an internal organization, it became clear that our collection of intellectual property, along with our technological and operational expertise, represented a significant value creation capacity. In to order make our knowledge and expertise available to companies outside of Shell, a significant part of this capability was placed on an independent, commercial footing. Thus, our charter then became to turn this internal expertise into a commercially viable operation and "pay our own way" as a profit center.

Today, our aim is to help raise our customer's business performance by combining leading-edge technology with extensive operating experience. The ability to team up with our customers is a critical component of this objective. While solving particular problems requires area-specific skills, effective business solutions often involve experts from different fields working together as a close-knit group. Jeff overviews one of these collaborative relationships in his book, our partnership with the Ferrari Formula 1 racing team, which provides a clear view into how this manifests in our customer relationships. Shell Global Solutions has worked hard to foster a collaborative culture and as a result, integrated teams, built around customers' requirements and combining their employees with ours, are a natural feature of our organization.

Achieving and sustaining profitable growth in today's highly competitive global market requires the essential ability to harness the full range and depth of expertise that lies within your organization. Products and even technology are quite easily replicated, but personal expertise, operational excellence, and customer intimacy are far more elusive and that is where your true differential lies.

Harnessing this tremendous source of value creation capacity is a great challenge. As we ourselves worked to accomplish this transformation in our business, we found that it involved three key tasks.

1. Technical experts, who deliver unquestioned excellence in service and support, have to be aligned with the entire organization around what it takes to shape a compelling value-based solution and most importantly what it takes to deliver it.
2. Learning how to sell the process and technology expertise, including intellectual property, is critical. For us, success required more than just "selling" our services; we needed to develop the structure and discipline to allow us to guide our customers through a process to recognize the value potential we offer. Jeff addresses this

issue and the need to "create the incentive to change" and the "confidence to invest" within the executive leadership of your customers. Customers must recognize and be willing to pay for the value delivered.

3. Finally, the business focus must shift from competing at the product or point solutions level, to the goal of being engaged as a "sole source" to our customers, capable of providing integrated solutions over time, in a mutually beneficial relationship. From our perspective, it is quite obvious that the current market is expanding the solution focus from improving the efficiency of a single process to finding ways of optimizing the entire value chain of a customer organization.

There are three key messages from Jeff's first book, *Mastering the Complex Sale,* that resonated with the direction I wanted to lead our business. In *The Prime Solution,* Jeff expands on these three points as they relate to responsibilities throughout the entire organization.

1. First, the customer does not have a decision process that is robust enough to match the complexity of the decisions that need to be made.

2. Second, the business of selling is not just about matching viable solutions to the customers that require them, it's also about managing the change process the customer will need to go through to implement the solution and achieve the value promised by the solution. One of the key differentiators of our position in the market is our attention to managing change and making change stick in our customers' organizations.

3. Third, it's not enough to merely propose value; we need to provide a detailed quantification of the value gap, thorough guidance and support during implementation

and finally, the ability to provide undeniable measurement of the value achieved.

Reading *The Prime Solution* confirmed the realization that we had been focusing too much of our attention on creating sales messages to our customers. We were making a strong case for why they should broaden their focus from improving efficiencies of process components to the optimization of the larger value chain, but, we also needed to ensure that we could deliver on our value promises.

The Prime Solution described what I and senior management needed to do internally to ensure that Shell Global Solutions could deliver on the value commitments we were making to customers. It provides the roadmap for integrating our organization in a multifaceted interaction with the customer and delivering on our promises. This multidisciplinary strategy proves especially valuable when providing consultancy services in business processes that extend across technology and business boundaries as well as geopolitical boundaries. It also reiterates some conclusions I have come to about customer value.

- *First, value should be added to the customer's entire business, not just a specific part of it.* Unless you consider the impact on your customers' businesses from end-to-end, savings made in one part of their business stand to be cancelled out by losses in another. For example, one part of their business might identify savings in working capital through a reduction of stock levels, only to find that this leads to raised levels at another point in the chain or, even worse, causes a decrease in their ability to serve their customers.
- *Second, the value created for your customer should be easily identified and owned by your customer.* It must be possible to measure the potential value that can be created for the customer and how the customer's business is impacted by the absence of that value. The executive team within your

customer's organization must be resolute in its belief of the value promised and its commitment to achieving it. Such a clear measurement strategy makes progress easy to track and generates the commitment necessary to deliver on any planned initiatives.

- *Third—and this is the major objective of Thull's* Prime Solutions—*the value you promise must be delivered.* It is very easy for customers to become overloaded with new improvement initiatives that fade out owing to lack of resources, poor planning, and the absence of buy-in from staff. Many will suggest that successful implementation and capturing value is the customer's responsibility, but as an internal organization, we never had the luxury of abdicating or even transferring responsibility for success. At Shell, we place considerable emphasis on change management, involving people at all levels in the organization, and on the development of firm and workable implementation plans that take into account the specific character, culture, and priorities of the organization. I cannot emphasize this point too much, and you will see that Jeff has clearly identified and articulated the critical role of change management in your success.

- *Fourth, the "secret sauce" is the heart and soul of your organization—the people!* It is easy to forget that despite advances in technology and business processes, people are still the prime factor in determining your success and your customers. As we progress in this dynamic business environment, roles and responsibilities will often evolve. In general, people must be given the opportunity to have a much better understanding of the business outside their own area. This will result in a greater accountability and responsibility for delivering on your value promises.

These are significant changes in how most of us "sell" value to our customers and they pose an interesting paradox: We can't hope to change how our customers perceive the value we offer until we change how we perceive that value.

We, as leaders, need to manage this change. We need to bring together the most suitable people in the first place, create an environment conducive to working, provide training and development, and establish efficient communications.

- We must provide our people with a broader understanding of business outside their own functional areas.
- We must realize that just as we cannot dictate change to our customers, we should also not dictate to our own staff, as well.
- We must provide our internal colleagues with the same level of attention and support we give our customers.

Leading-edge companies continually improve their business performance by taking a fresh look at the value challenge. Value-based innovation is the key to long-term business success and it is heavily dependent on better business processes, access to more consistent and up-to-the-minute information, and the highest utilization of the expertise of the professionals who carry out the activities that make up the value chain. *The Prime Solution* is a sound guide to this work. It presents an innovative approach to customer value and offers a compelling look at how you can assure your organization's ability to consistently create and deliver value for your customers and capture a premium share of that value for your organization. Innovation is the key to long-term business success. Jeff Thull will stimulate your thinking and provide you with a solid template that will guide your strategy as you continue to address the ongoing challenges of today's evolving business environment.

Greg Lewin, President
Shell Global Solutions International BV
The Hague, The Netherlands

Shell Global Solutions is a dynamic service organization with one main aim—to help customers raise their business performance. Combining leading-edge technology with extensive operating experience, Shell Global Solutions provides innovative and practical solutions that are designed to help companies achieve their full potential.

THE PRIME SOLUTION IMPERATIVE

If your company is competing in today's business-to-business solutions marketplace, creating and capturing value is likely a critical component of your corporate strategy. You are a value seller. Your company is working hard to *create* value-laden solutions. You strive to ensure that your customers can *comprehend* the value that your solutions deliver. And your successful efforts to gain and retain customers who are willing to *compensate* you for that value are vital to a financially viable business.

This is challenging work in a growing economy and an even more substantial challenge in today's volatile markets. Simply put, most solutions are losing propositions for both sellers and buyers. Here's how McKinsey & Company calculated the odds of success:

> "Solutions selling" has been all the rage for the last 5 to 10 years, yet 75 percent of the companies that attempt to offer solutions fail to return the cost of their investment.[1]

Among the many reasons for this discouraging success rate is the fierce competition between solution sellers. It is difficult to identify a solution market that is not inundated with value promises—promises that almost all look and sound alike to customers. It is very difficult to differentiate solutions, when all the competitors can and are using the same words to describe their value propositions. Further, when customers finally do choose between competing solutions, they have an extraordinarily difficult time achieving the value they believe they were promised and rightfully expect.

In fact, statistics show that customers fail to achieve the value they anticipated in over half of all complex solution purchases.

The 75 percent of solution providers who fail to cover their costs, and the better than one in two customers who never achieve the value they purchased, are falling into the Value Gap. The Value Gap is the seemingly unbridgeable space between the complex, value-laden solutions that sellers work so hard to create and the results that their customers actually achieve. It is like a vicious vacuum, sucking present and future solution profits out of the businesses of both sellers and their customers.

Recent, notable solution failures are the primary reason that customers increasingly demand solutions that come with something more concrete than just a promise of value. They are demanding *clear* answers, *attainable* solutions, and *tangible* performance improvement roadmaps in the struggle to address the challenges and problems they are facing.

Meeting these customer demands requires solutions that you

- deliver optimal results, capable of leveraging value to the highest level of the customer's business.
- ensure that the customer has identified and purchased the best answer to their problems.
- provide solution implementation and value enhancement strategies that enable customers to achieve the ROI that they anticipated.

We call robust solutions that successfully meet these requirements Prime Solutions. Prime Solutions beat the substantial odds of solution failure and deliver maximum value to both sellers and their customers.

INTRODUCING PRIME SOLUTIONS

Prime Solutions embrace an extended vision of value accountability that allows the organizations providing them to differentiate their companies and offerings in today's marketplaces and in customers' minds. As we will see, they also represent a significant and attractive opportunity to create and build sustainable success as a solution provider.

Prime Solutions achieve these goals by incorporating three protocols: value maximization, decision acuity, and return optimization.

1. *Value maximization* is the application of your company's value capabilities to the highest level within your customer's organization. Complex solutions can deliver benefits to customers at three levels of value: product, process, and performance. Prime Solutions affect all three levels with a cumulative impact that reaches the performance level. They enable your customers to serve their customers better, they provide distinct and measurable competitive differentiation, and they assist your customers in expanding their businesses. Thus, in the customer's mind, the Prime Solution seller is a distinct source of competitive advantage.

2. *Decision acuity* is the provision of the knowledge and the process that enables customers to recognize the tangible value that your solutions can provide. Your customers can fix an accurate cost on the absence of that value, then determine the overall financial impact of your solutions. Decision processes in the complex solutions world are defined at three levels: reactive, proactive, and interactive. The decision processes that accompany Prime Solutions operate at the interactive level, at which the solution provider delivers a precise, collaborative process that empowers the customer to reach optimal

decisions continuously. Thus, in the customer's mind, the Prime Solution provider is a valued colleague as well as a trusted advisor.

3. *Return optimization* is the delivery of implementation strategies and postsale support that enable customers to implement complex solutions successfully, measure ROI, and achieve and enhance value. Implementation strategies are defined at three levels: purchase, installation, and results. Again, Prime Solutions affect all three levels, finding their cumulative impact at the results level, where the solution provider actively participates in implementing the solution and ensures the successful delivery of the promised outcomes. Thus, in the customer's mind, the Prime Solution seller becomes a critical, if not strategic, business partner.

BECOMING A PRIME SOLUTION PROVIDER

A Prime Solution is *not* created and delivered by any one function within the organization. Leveraging the value inherent in a solution, a high-quality decision process, and a successful implementation requires a crossfunctional effort. It involves intimacy and collaboration between the R&D, marketing, sales, and service/support functions within the provider's company as well as an equal level of collaboration between the provider's team and the customer's team. Further, optimizing the effectiveness of their joint efforts requires that the functions communicate using a common language and process.

The Prime Solution Cycle encompasses the systems, skills, and disciplines that lie behind Prime Solutions. Some solution providers, like those profiled in this book, will already be conversant with some or all of these. For others, creating and delivering Prime Solutions will represent a considerable leap forward.

The establishment of the Prime Solution Cycle typically requires a redeployment of resources, a restructuring of functional interactions, and, most of all, a new customercentric culture driven by a singular mindset and language. Before you back down from the challenge, think about how you would react to a company that brought such a solution to your door. This solution would positively and clearly impact your business performance and profitability. This solution provider would not only ensure that you designed and selected the best solution for your hard-earned dollars but would also help you achieve a successful implementation—and, further, help maximize and measure your return on investment. This vendor is a Prime Resource, and all companies struggle to occupy that position in their customers' minds.

MOVING FORWARD

This book was written to guide and assist business-to-business solution sellers in their quest for long-term growth, competitive dominance, and profitability through Prime Solutions. Toward that end, the book is organized into three parts that echo and elaborate upon this introduction.

1. *Part One* explores the environment in which today's complex solutions must compete. It maps the parameters and ramifications of the challenges facing businesses today, traces the evolution of the business-to-business marketplace through three eras of value deterioration, and identifies the barriers that stymie professionals in their attempts to bridge the Value Gap. Part One takes a hard look at complex solutions and finds that, by most measures, value achievement is relatively rare. This conclu-

sion is disappointing, but it reveals a highly attractive opportunity for businesses that can deliver on their value promises.

2. *Part Two* translates the demands of today's complex solution markets into protocols that define and inform Prime Solutions. It details what it means for a solution to leverage value, to ensure that the customer makes a quality decision to invest, to create implementation guidance and support its guarantee that customers achieve the value promised, and to preempt competitive threats by providing continuous value enhancement. Part Two paints a detailed portrait of complex solutions that are capable of meeting and exceeding the challenges inherent in today's business-to-business marketplace.

3. *Part Three* answers the question: How can my company develop and deliver Prime Solutions? It explores the organizational mindset, capabilities, and work processes within Prime Solution organizations. It describes the strategies and techniques that drive the development, marketing, sales, and service/support of Prime Solutions. Part Three follows the Prime Solution's evolutionary process from genesis to successful implementation.

I hope that this book will help you give form and substance to the marketplace trends, customer demands, and competitive pressures that you and your company confront every day. I further hope that it will encourage you to pursue and deliver improved value promises and that you receive the rewards that accrue to successful solution providers, today's Prime Resources. If this book helps illuminate the path to Prime Solutions, then it has delivered on its value promise.

In June of 1981, I decided to enter the consulting business. It is a story too long to even attempt to make short. Suffice it to say, I selected sales and marketing as a practice focus because I thought I knew how to market and sell. I said "thought I knew" because as I began to work with clients to chronicle their top performers and best practices, I quickly began to learn how much I didn't know. I first and foremost must acknowledge the hundreds of sales and marketing professionals, along with their R&D, manufacturing, technical support, and service colleagues, who have been creating and delivering "Prime Solutions" long before we coined the phrase and documented processes to describe their work.

During the past 23 years, many of those individuals have become close friends with a shared passion for their customers and their companies. I want to express a thank-you to a group of special clients and colleagues who were so passionate about this project that they invested their valuable time and expertise to review the early drafts of this book: Jane Blinde, Richard Brooks, Donny Holender, Randy Hull, Michael Liacko, Stan Luboda, Dave Madsen, Dave Millman, Charlie Morris, Nido Qubein, Peter Muldowney, Judy Robinson, and John Sullivan. Their comments and suggestions were insightful, challenging, and greatly added to the strength of the content and the utility I'm sure you will experience when reading and applying our suggestions.

As you read, you'll find references to many noted authors. I wish to thank them for the clarity their research has added to the concepts and strategies we are describing and I know will assist you in understanding and implementing the Prime Solution within your business.

I would also like to thank the executives who gave their time and shared their perspectives on their successful approaches to creating and delivering whole solutions: Peter Boler, Jeff Bolke, Richard Brooks, Jim Clouser, Dan DiCarlo, Darren Fish, Wayne Hutchinson, Bill Graham, Dave Madsen, Mike Maples, Kevin McPoyle, and Rick Urschel.

I am very grateful to Greg Lewin for contributing his views to the foreword. As we began to work with Shell Global Solutions, it was quite apparent that Greg's vision was clearly in alignment with our philosophy, and the team he and Wayne Hutchinson have put together was already quite successful in creating and delivering Prime Solutions to the customers.

My thanks to my agent John Willig of Literary Services who guided us as we shaped this book from its earliest conceptual form and carried our message to the publishing world. The clarity of writing you will experience must be attributed to the highly talented team of Ted and Donna Kinni. They have been able to take mountains of information, research, and consulting experiences (picture tax receipts and shoeboxes) and bring them together in a book that brings this critical issue to life and lays it and its solution out in a very compelling and comprehensible fashion.

Equally as difficult as the task of transferring these concepts and examples to a book is the challenge of translating the same into consulting procedures and performance development seminars and workshops. I am greatly indebted to the instructional design talents of John Sullivan.

I am uniquely and significantly blessed to have Pat Thull as my partner in business and in marriage. As our good friend, Michael McKinley, constantly reminds me: "You have managed to marry significantly above yourself." Not only did I marry above myself, but I found that unique partner in business who can lead, balance, inspire, be someone to lean on, and most of all clarify and implement some of the half-baked ideas I have come up with. As I believe is critical in an ideal partnership, we have compensating strengths. Pat provides me with an incredible amount of insight and support. Her wisdom and insight can be found throughout this book. As COO of Prime Resource Group, her guidance of both the Prime team and our customers' teams has supported the significant success our clients have achieved in developing and delivering their Prime Solutions.

I also would like to thank our children. As your children are growing up, you accept your responsibility to nurture and guide their development, but you may not expect how much you will learn from your children. As they now have all entered their adult lives, I have become more of a learner than teacher. I've been able to watch Jennifer pursue her dream of becoming an emergency pediatrician. She has just completed her fellowship and I've had the privilege of following her medical education. What I have learned from Jennifer about the medical profession has been of enormous value in modeling the education of business professionals. Jessica has completed her Masters in Social Service Administration. I've learned so much from Jessica's passion for children and her studies in human behavior and counseling. She is a school social worker, working with preschool children and their families, for the Head Start program in a major city. She is impacting children's lives in a wonderful way. Our many conversations about human behavior, motivation, and change management have been instructional for me, reinforcing and refining the many concepts that we bring to our clients. Brian shares my interest in motor sports and has shown me what real passion and dedication looks like. He has been drawing and designing vehicles since he was 2 years old and devouring automotive magazines since he was 7. He has poured every spare dollar into his cars since he was 16 and is now taking that passion and turning it towards his own business—doing performance, appearance, and audio/video system modifications to high-end vehicles. Our three children inspire us daily with their energy and their passion for life.

I feel enormously privileged to be able to express what we have learned in our consulting practice in this book and trust that it will be instructional and perhaps it can even hit the level of inspirational as you go about enhancing your personal and professional success. My thanks to Michael Cunningham and the team at Dearborn Trade Publishing for bringing this book to the market.

Part One

SWALLOWED UP IN THE VALUE GAP

The Value Gap: the high-cost disconnect between the value that products and services are designed to deliver to customers and the value that customers actually achieve.

How big is the Gap? Studies and statistics suggest that over half of all the complex or whole solutions sold in today's sophisticated, diverse business-to-business marketplace do not live up to their promise in customers' eyes.

Are you in danger of being swallowed up in the Value Gap? You may be if your company is experiencing symptoms like these:

- Your sales force can't deliver or sustain pricing levels for your complex products and services that will provide adequate returns.
- The sales cycle is chaotic and increasing in length and cost.
- Forecasting results and planning for the future is increasingly difficult.
- Customer satisfaction and retention rates are dropping.
- You are unable to capitalize on lucrative opportunities for expanding current customer relationships. Customers claim to recognize value creation at the outset, but in the end, they will not pay for it.

1

THE ELUSIVE PRIME SOLUTION

We all know that customers do not buy complex products and services; they buy outcomes. They buy business results. Thirty years ago, Peter Drucker flatly stated in his encyclopedic *Management: Tasks, Responsibilities, Practices,* "The customer never buys a product. By definition, the customer buys the satisfaction of a want. He buys value." Drucker criticized the corporations of the 1970s for ignoring value from the customer's perspective. "What is value to the customer?" he wrote. "It may be the most important question. Yet it is the one least often asked."[1]

What "wants" do business-to-business customers try to satisfy? The things that were of value to them in 1974, and are still of value today, are exactly the same things that you value in your business—increased revenues, lower costs, more efficient and resilient operations, and optimal employee productivity. Most importantly, just like you, your customers want to establish and expand profitable, long-term relationships with their customers. In short, they want *solutions* to the problems and competitive challenges that they face in the battle for corporate success.

Twenty years after Drucker's opus was published, Lou Gerstner based his dramatic turnaround of IBM on the concept of solutions. In a real sense, Gerstner's strategy represented a return to IBM's roots. In the 1940s and 1950s, Thomas Watson, Sr. drove IBM's growth with a hybrid product/service model. He understood that IBM's customers did not want electronic accounting machines. They wanted the information and efficiencies that the machines enabled. So IBM leased equipment and focused on delivering the value. His son, Thomas Watson, Jr., embraced the computer but kept the same business model. By the 1960s, IBM was a multibillion-dollar company. Watson, Jr., who served as CEO until 1971 and on the executive committee until 1979, wrote:

> We are one business and, for the most part, a business with a single mission. Our job, and that of each division, is to help customers solve their problems through the use of data processing systems and other information handling equipment."[2]

Unfortunately, the 1980s proved to be a watershed era in the company's history. As the competition in the computer industry grew and the PC emerged, IBM started to look like a dinosaur. Instead of creating solutions based on the emerging needs of customers, it focused even more intensely on selling its existing products. In 1992, the company shocked the business world by declaring a $4.97 billion loss, at that time one of the largest in corporate history.

IBM had become a moribund giant when Gerstner, an accomplished executive but hardly a high-tech insider, was hired as CEO in March of 1993. At that time, most of IBM's managers and employees saw their company as what Gerstner describes as a "piece part" manufacturer.

Gerstner was confounded by attitudes that he found in his new company and industry. In his book about the IBM turnaround, *Who Says Elephants Can't Dance?*, Gerstner wrote:

> I just wish every one of these incredibly bright technologists could spend a year as a customer and see the different viewpoint customers have about computing technology. They would see that customers find technology very difficult to integrate into everyday lives and enterprises. They would find the promises overblown and the returns more difficult than promised. They would find that, at the end of the day, many of the critical decisions that managers, employees, and consumers have to make either have no relationship to technology, or they just may find that technology can actually be an impediment."[3]

From his firsthand experiences as a business-to-business buyer of IT systems, Gerstner knew that customers in IBM's markets had little or no interest in the hardware and software of information technology. To them, these were simply commodities. Just like any business-to-business buyer, IBM's customers wanted solutions to their business problems and challenges, solutions that delivered on the value promised.

Accordingly, that is where Gerstner focused his attention. He took a subsidiary unit of IBM's sales force, Integrated Systems Services Corporation, and transformed it into IBM Global Services. The expanded aim of the new business unit was to deliver integrated IT services to customers—whole solutions that ranged from system definition and construction to providing fully outsourced operations.

The decision turned out to be extremely savvy. Global Services, in fact, quickly became the driver of IBM's recovery and the company's fastest growing business, contributing 80 percent of total revenue growth during Gerstner's tenure.

"Had the effort to build IBM Global Services failed, IBM— or at least my vision of IBM—would have failed with it," Gerstner declared. "In 1992, services was a $7.4 billion business at IBM (excluding maintenance). In 2001, it had risen to a $30 billion business and accounted for roughly half of our workforce."[4]

In its post-Gerstner era, IBM continued to pursue a solution-driven strategy. Gerstner's successor, Sam Palmisano, supported and extended the gains of Global Services by purchasing PricewaterhouseCoopers's consulting arm for $3.5 billion.

THE MAJOR RISK IN MARKETING SOLUTIONS

Given the results of IBM and other successful solution providers, it should be no surprise that most of today's business-to-business sellers are in hot pursuit of whole solutions that can satisfy the customer wants described above. Certainly, the business-to-business sector is awash in sophisticated, painstakingly differentiated solutions, all of which, their sellers assure customers, hold great promise. Just browse through the advertisements in a recent issue of any trade business magazine and see the declarations of product and service performance.

One enormous problem, however, isn't mentioned in any of the ads. All too often, customers are unable to achieve the value promises that accompany these solutions. Marketers often ignore this elephant of a problem—at great cost to their credibility. Customers, on the other hand, are fully aware of the wide and often unbridgeable gap between advertising promises and actual value achievement. The CRM (customer relationship management) marketplace provides a good example. CRM is a hot concept, one of the few that experienced continued demand through the economic downturn of the early 2000s, and myriad CRM-related products and services are finding eager corporate buyers. But how many of those buyers are realizing the value they rightly anticipated when they purchased CRM solutions?

In a recent survey, Gartner, Inc., reported that failure rates for CRM implementations were running as high as 65 percent. Giga Information Group reported CRM failure rates in the 60 to 70 percent range, and Insight Technology found that more than two-thirds of CRM projects failed to produce meaningful improvement in company revenues.

The need for customers to undertake repeated CRM implementations before they achieve the value they were promised is so typical that a senior editor at *CRM* magazine felt justified in giving the problem a name and a cover story.

> Anyone who has gone through one CRM rollout knows what a complicated undertaking it can be," wrote Lisa Picarille. "But imagine a company implementing CRM a second time, or even a third. In fact, organizations completing three rollouts are so common that we call the experience the Goldilocks Syndrome, taking our cue from the children's story, "Goldilocks and the Three Bears:" the first time the system was too big, the second time too small, and finally the third time it is just right.[5]

Picarille profiled three companies that had experienced repeated failures in the quest to implement CRM solutions. Each company was forced to purchase multiple solutions and repeatedly reinvest resources, time, and effort before achieving the value promised by their vendors.

You might conclude from this that the CRM problem is insurmountable and should be avoided, but that would be both unrealistic and a mistake. CRM isn't to blame. If you look back over the past decade or so, you can find similar failure rates for a host of valuable and proven business concepts. Solutions associated with total quality management, business process reengineering, information technology, manufacturing resource planning, e-business, and enterprise resource planning have all experienced high failure rates.

In the mid-1990s, business process reengineering (BPR) initiatives often ended in embarrassment. "BPR implementations fail 50 percent to 70 percent of the time. A failed implementation is one that fails completely or does not yield expected increases in productivity and quality," reported Dr. Michael Wells of Minnesota State University.[6]

Enterprise resource planning (ERP) implementations have recorded similar failure rates as well as public flameouts at companies such as Hershey Foods and Nike. In October 1999, Hershey Foods announced that a $112 million ERP implementation, using SAP applications and IBM consultants, had caused shipment delays and incomplete order delivery during its busy Halloween sales season. The result of this missed value release was a 19 percent drop in third-quarter profits.[7]

In March 2001, Nike announced that a flawed implementation of a $400 million ERP system, including i2 Technologies applications, was partially to blame for its quarterly profit shortfalls. The resulting problems included product shortages in some lines, overproduction in others, and late deliveries.[8] The value at risk was substantial.

In another high profile case, the Internal Revenue Service has been struggling to modernize its tax file-keeping system, now four decades old. "Most taxpayers are younger than the computer system that the IRS relies on to maintain its master files on individuals and companies," reported David Cay Johnson in the *New York Times.* Further, "A collapse is inevitable without a new system, because the few people who could keep the old system functioning are close to retiring."

Unfortunately, the IRS has already experienced two modernization failures at a cost exceeding $4 billion. In December 2003, the IRS Oversight Board announced that the $8 billion modernization effort currently being run by Computer Sciences Corporation (CSC) is 40 percent over budget and as much as 27 months behind schedule. The Board also publicly warned CSC that it would be replaced "if significant improvements are not demonstrated quickly."[9]

As I'm sure you'll note, these solution failures are by no means the exclusive domain of the technology industry. We could go on and on with examples from pharmaceutical, automotive, professional services, manufacturing, chemicals, etc. All have similar stories of value placed at risk and subsequently lost. The critical point is that too many companies and institutions are making substantial investments in whole solutions aimed at satisfying their wants—meeting organizational challenges and solving problems—and yet are not achieving their goals. These organizations are purchasing solutions that promise value, are devoting time and effort to capturing that value, and still are coming up empty-handed. The value they purchased is only partially achieved or not achieved at all. In our technology savvy marketplace, how can this be happening?

THE CAUSES OF SOLUTION FAILURE

When you study individual solution failure cases, you find that the seemingly unique circumstances that combine to sabotage the successful fulfillment of value usually fall into one of three broad categories.

1. Value is not achieved because the product or service itself is unable to deliver on the promise made.
2. Value is not achieved because the customer is unable to properly implement the product and service.
3. Value is not achieved because the customer's expectations have not been met.

These are the major reasons why complex products and services—the kinds of solutions that are developed, marketed, sold, and supported by companies in industries such as software, medical devices and equipment, IT solutions, industrial chemicals, manufacturing systems, professional and financial services—fail to deliver on the promise of their value.

Value is not achieved because the product or service itself is unable to deliver on the promise.

In other words, the solution is flawed.

This failure can be attributed to qualities inherent in the solution. Consider how often early releases of software solutions are simply not ready for market. When sellers do not properly design and develop their products and services, no amount of acrobatics can coax value from them.

A solution may also be unable to deliver value because it is not properly matched to the customer's actual problem or challenge and the broader business areas involved. Complex solutions are not paper clips. They address complex problems that are difficult to analyze and often feature parameters that are unique to a specific customer. That is why mismatches between problems and solutions are so common. Like a medication, a solution that is improperly prescribed may work, in the literal sense of the word, but still do great harm if the complete impact is not accurately understood.

The value is not achieved because the customer is unable to implement the product and service properly.

In this case, we have a solution that could work in the customer's situation, but for one of a variety of reasons, it is never implemented to the full degree of its ROI potential.

The problem could be technical, such as integration and compatibility issues. The customer may have the expertise needed to implement and utilize the solution, but existing processes, such as intercompany policies or systems, may negate its value. Think about the compatibility issues that crop up when installing new hardware or software on a single computer, then multiply them by a thousand. Implementation problems may also stem from cultural considerations. Managers and employees often refuse to accept new solutions out of normal resistance to change. Often heard: "That's not how we do things around here."

With increasing frequency, we suspect, well-intentioned solution providers, because of cost pressures imposed by senior management during longer implementation cycles, often fail to sustain the needed resources required to support a customer's whole solution implementation.

Every buying decision is a decision to change, and every solution implementation is about executing that change. Complex solutions often require complex, fundamental changes in the way a customer does business, and as Kotter showed in his seminal work *Leading Change*,[10] it is incredibly difficult to successfully undertake and accomplish organizational change. As he states, "in too many situations the improvements have been disappointing and the carnage has been appalling . . . the anguish we've witnessed in the past decade *is* avoidable." In short, the customer is not prepared to manage the change and thus a tremendous amount of value is lost.

The value is not achieved because the customer's expectations have not been met.

Finally, we see situations where solutions work and are considered successfully installed or delivered by the seller, yet the customer still does not achieve the value they expected.

Solution failures in this category are most often caused when the seller overinflates a solution's expected value or never understands the customer's value expectations. When a salesperson leads a customer to expect a 50 percent reduction in costs, but the solution delivers a 25 percent reduction, the customer may rightfully consider the solution a failure. After all, the investment was based on a return that never materialized.

In a second, more paradoxical situation, which occurs more frequently than you might expect, the customer does not fully comprehend the value delivered and, consequently, declares the solution a failure. This happens, for instance, when a customer is not supported with the means to realize and measure the improvements brought about by the solution.

Although value fulfillment has actually occurred in this final category of solution failures, value—like beauty—is in the eye of the beholder. If the customer doesn't perceive that the expected value has been delivered, the seller incurs the same consequences as if it had delivered an actual solution failure.

THE IMPACT OF FAILED SOLUTIONS

Because businesses that sell complex, value-laden products and services are often reluctant to face the reality and causes of solution failure, the impact of those failures on their own performance and bottom line goes largely unrecognized and unaddressed. Ignorance, however, is not bliss. It puts companies in a very vulnerable, high-risk situation in their highly competitive business-to-business markets.

Typically, a solution failure sets off an aggressive round in the blame game. The customer points an accusing finger at the seller and the solution and claims, "It doesn't work as promised." The seller points back at the buyer, saying, "Our solution works; the failure was caused by your inability to properly implement and utilize it."

Who is responsible for solution failures? For the seller, the only correct answer is: *It doesn't matter.* No matter what the outcome of the blame game, the situation is no-win. Unfortunately, whether the buyer or the seller is responsible for the solution failure, the seller will bear a significant, negative impact. In a market where renewable and sustainable relationships are critical to the bottom line, there is no room for failure.

For starters, the relationship with the customer will be severely strained, if not terminated. Few customers will shoulder the full burden of a solution failure, and the overwhelming majority will not completely absolve a vendor who has not delivered on value promises. A fundamental tenet of human behavior holds that people will externalize blame to protect their own well being. In business, this means that vendors will end up with the short straw, as customers have the advantage of holding the money.

The sale itself will be threatened, as in CSC's $8 billion contract with the IRS. The customer's trust becomes impaired; subsequently, the equitable resolution of the current problem and the prospect for future sales is problematic. In worst-case scenarios, legal battles over liability cast a looming shadow.

Whether or not lawyers make a formal appearance, the impact of solution failures inevitably spreads into the marketplace. Unhappy customers spread the word. Studies suggest that, on average, an unhappy customer tells nine other people about their experience; 13 percent of unhappy customers pass on the negative commentary to more than 20 other people.[11]

These figures are a drop in the bucket compared to the damage that can occur if the customer decides to go public. Now, the blame game is exponentially magnified, as the hard-won brand recognition and corporate reputation of the seller becomes damaged. Also, keep in mind that, for every well-publicized failure, there are numerous situations where the customer is not happy with the value received and does nothing more than put the seller in the category with all other competitors—not to be trusted—continuing the downward pricing spiral of commoditization.

Whether right or wrong, when Nike pointed to i2 Technologies as one cause of its poor quarterly performance, it unleashed an avalanche of negative publicity on the solution seller. I2 Technologies president Greg Brady felt compelled to defend his company publicly. The headline in *Information Week* read: "Nike Just Didn't Do It Right, Says i2 Technologies: Vendor Says Company Ignored Deployment Advice, and It's Not to Blame for Sales Shortfall." Brady was now in the unenviable position of feeding the fire in a story that was bringing the efficacy of its products into question *and* risking public scrutiny by contradicting a major customer.[12]

Existing and prospective customers get very uneasy when they read stories like these. This is exactly what happened in the Hershey case cited earlier. The leader of an ERP implementation at Lockheed Martin called SAP "to find out what makes my implementation different." SAP cochairman Hasso Plattner ended up making a public statement, telling *ComputerWorld,* "Ninety-nine percent of our customers are happy." SAP, he said, "did a good implementation, and it's not our fault." He also admitted the resulting negative impact on his company. "Prospects ask, 'Am I the next one on the list?'"[13]

All of these consequences have a direct impact on the financial results of the selling firm. Current customer relationships may be threatened or lost, margins are squeezed as the seller responds to the problem, and the lifetime value of the customer is reduced. As the word spreads, the impact is felt through loss of market share and the increase in sales cycle time and accompanying escalation in the cost of sales. Prospective customers are much more skeptical of vendors who have been the subject of bad publicity, rightfully earned or not. Established customers demand assurances that they won't experience the same poor results and expect a compromise through a reduction in cost, which puts a tighter squeeze on margins.

HIDDEN OPPORTUNITY IN THE VALUE GAP

Because value fulfillment is so elusive, frustration and animosity are the two most common emotions in the whole-solutions marketplace. Frustration and animosity are stifling the business-to-business sector.

Solution providers are frustrated and angry when they can't translate the differentiated products and services that they have worked so hard to create into bottom-line profitability. Their customers are frustrated and angry when they don't achieve the benefits and return on investment that they expected—and have often been explicitly promised.

This tense space between sellers and buyers is the Value Gap—the gap between the promise of value and its ultimate fulfillment. Solution sellers and their customers end up on opposite sides of the gap. They blame each other for creating it, while the ramifications of the problem can sabotage the efforts of both of their businesses and the entire industry.

That is the gray cloud, but where is the silver lining? Because the complex solutions marketplace, in a wide variety of industries, is underserved and value-hungry, it holds opportunity for companies like IBM that can learn to identify, manage, and close the Value Gap. This book is about bringing to market complex products and services that not only won't get swallowed up in the Value Gap but also will provide a precise connection to your customers' value requirements. This value achievement process is disciplined and structured, a whole-solutions approach that mitigates the risk of diluting value as it is translated throughout your organization and to your customers' bottom line.

We call these products and services Prime Solutions. Such a solution—no matter its individual characteristics and market niche—contains a specific set of protocols that enables customers to achieve the full promise of its value. Companies that strive to create and sell Prime Solutions adopt rigorous organizational processes and competencies that ensure these protocols are properly designed, delivered, and measured.

A Prime Solution is a metamodel and, to some extent, an ideal. But it is, nevertheless, an ideal that is attainable and practical. There are companies that are bucking the odds of solution failure and working hard to approach the Prime Solution ideal. Their business results reflect their efforts. Even small and midsized companies, who don't have the resources of the *Fortune* 1,000, are using this model to provide a clear path to ensure value achievement for their customers.

One company in pursuit of Prime Solutions is Waters Corporation, an analytical instrumentation developer located in Milford, Massachusetts. Waters is the global leader in three analytical technologies—high performance liquid chromatography, mass spectrometry, and thermal analysis.

The company was founded 45 years ago as a research boutique, developing and building one-of-a-kind instruments in response to customer requests. In the early 1960s, Waters began producing instruments for the life sciences markets, but it retained the closeness to the customer in the development process that had informed its product strategies for the first few years. Today, customer collaboration in the design and R&D process ensures open communication of customer business requirements and continues to drive a development process that has produced more new products in the past three years than in any five-year period in the company's history.

Waters is firmly focused on the value its customers achieve. The company knows that its customers do not buy an instrument for its own sake; they are buying the results that an instrument is designed to measure. Accordingly, while others in its industry have chosen to cut costs by outsourcing services, Waters created the Waters Connections Program, a portfolio of service and support programs that are managed and delivered by its own trained and certified specialists. Customers get more than a service technician; they get a professional who understands the experiment being run and helps to ensure the accuracy of its results.

Waters nearly tripled its sales from $332 million in 1995 to a record $958 million in 2003. When it celebrated its 45th anniversary that year, Waters earned recognition on *Business 2.0's* annual "B2 100" list of the fastest-growing technology companies and *IndustryWeek's* "Top 50 U.S. Performers" list. In June 2004, a *Forbes* magazine study depicted Waters as the second most successful large IPO between 1993 and 2003, with a return of 1,051 percent.

Another company that creates Prime Solutions is The Graham Company, a Philadelphia-based commercial property and casualty insurance broker. Founded in 1950, Graham is the 47th largest insurance broker in the United States, reporting an annual premium volume of $200 million. Yet it maintains a sales force that is less than 10 percent of its 135 employees and generates its premiums from only 200 corporate clients. (Its nearest competitors in terms of annual premium volume, the brokers in the 46th and 48th positions, have close to 2,000 clients.)

Essentially, Graham has turned the traditional commercial insurance sales process on its head by transforming standardized insurance products into Prime Solutions. Toward that goal, the company invests in a rigorous process of new client discovery and the diagnosis of risk. In 2003, the professionals at Graham began discussions with 350 prospective clients. After those initial discussions, the company decided to pursue a relationship with only 35 companies and earned the business of 28 of them. When prospective clients agree to participate in the Graham process, the broker sends a team, which can include attorneys, risk managers, CPAs, and experts, into the prospective customer's business. It evaluates business and insurance issues and exposures, often finding 80 to 90 gaps in their current coverage. The gaps can include excess coverage as well as underinsured exposures and opportunities to self-insure. This work, for which consultants charge as much as $75,000, is provided without charge as part of Graham's diagnostic process.

In an industry that pursues volume sales of standardized products, Graham focuses on designing customized policies that deliver high value to the customer. It approaches insurance as a strategic component of the customer's business rather than as a standard overhead cost, and it creates tailored legal, technical, and financial packages designed to reflect each customer's unique insurance needs. It works hard to ensure that customers obtain maximum value for every insurance dollar spent. For instance, the company renegotiates standard insurance clauses and wording with providers, often eliminating loopholes in coverage at no additional cost to its customer.

Graham also remains committed to creating new value for established customers through the continual alignment of risk-management strategies with the customers' business objectives on "a daily basis, year-round." The company seeks to manage the customer's insurance requirements by, for example, reviewing the insurance issues of proposed acquisitions. It also maintains a 25-employee, in-house claims department to ensure rapid and proper reimbursement. The Graham Group has done a thorough job of identifying the sources of value within their capabilities, diagnosing their customers' uses of value, and managing the risks of achieving that value within their clients' organizations.

How well does this business strategy work? The numbers tell the story: Graham enjoys an 80+ percent conversion rate in an industry with a 15 percent average and maintains a 98 percent customer retention rate.

A third company that is succeeding with Prime Solutions is Motive, Inc., a service management software company based in Austin, Texas. Motive's software applications and suites enable companies such as Hewlett-Packard, EMC, British Telecom, 3Com, and Verizon Broadband to deliver and manage service processes, such as the initiation of service and the automated diagnosis of customer problems, remotely to their customers.

One reason why Motive's solutions can be considered Prime is because they enable customers to expand the value they deliver to their customers. At Verizon Broadband, for instance, the Motive Smart Virtual Assistant offers Verizon's customers a downloadable solution that gives them 24/7 access to self-service diagnosis and repair. Hundreds of thousands of Verizon's high-speed Internet customers have downloaded the Virtual Assistant. Thus, Motive adds value to its customers' business performance.

Moreover, Motive is explicitly focused on the value its customers derive from its solutions. It is the only service infrastructure software company with a "customer care" organization that is dedicated to working with customers beyond initial deployment to expand on the value achieved. In fact, Motive tracks the value delivered by its solutions within its customers' operations.

Founded in 1997 and funded by venture capitalists and private investors, Motive has rapidly grown into a $100 million company. In 2003, it was ranked 31st on the *Inc. 500* list of America's fastest growing companies, and it completed a successful initial public offering in June of 2004.

We'll hear more about all three of these companies later in this book. But, before we examine the protocols that inform the design of Prime products and services (the focus of Part Two) and the organizational prerequisites that enable their creation and implementation (the focus of Part Three), we need a deeper understanding of why failure is so pervasive in the complex solutions marketplace. We need to understand the barriers that often stand between value promises and their fulfillment. Toward that end, Chapter 2 explores the long-term development of the Value Gap and its current parameters, and Chapter 3 describes the five common barriers that sellers encounter in their drive toward value fulfillment.

2

THREE ERAS OF
VALUE DILUTION

Radical changes jolt us out of complacency and demand attention, but slow changes creep up, pass by, and, too often, leave us behind. The evolution of the Value Gap is the story of a new market environment created by a steady escalation of capabilities, requirements, and expectations. The result of this slow change is seen, but the underlying causes are not well understood or articulated. It is reminiscent of the old story of the frog that boils to death because it doesn't perceive the gradual heating of the water.

If the Value Gap had occurred overnight, we would have no trouble detecting it, its causes, and the solution. However, the current epidemic of the Value Gap has been evolving slowly, increasing in frequency and size for several decades or more.

The evolution of the Value Gap has been driven by the ever-changing definition of *value*. Sellers have always made value promises, both explicit and implicit, to buyers. The development pattern of those promises over the past 20 to 30 years is usually characterized by the term *added value*.

Through innovation and technological advances, business-to-business solution sellers strive to add value to their products and services in their race to gain competitive advantage. The linkage between innovation and business success is well established and widely accepted. In the early 1950s, Peter Drucker defined innovation as one of only two basic functions of a business enterprise (with marketing being the other). Fifty years later, today's thought leaders continue to define and study innovation as the driving force in corporate competitiveness and growth. A notable example is Harvard Business School's Clayton Christiensen, who pegged successful corporate growth to the management of two types of innovation: sustaining and disruptive.[1] Sustaining innovation is the evolution of a new version of an existing product or service; disruptive innovation is the creation of a new technology that supplants a previous one.

The enhancement of value through technological innovation is a good thing, a necessity for growth, but solution sellers tend to forget that it also leads to added complexity for all involved. This fact leads directly to the crux of the problem:

> At the same time that they are adding value to their products and services, they are also often making it more difficult for customers to understand, evaluate, implement, and achieve the full value that can be derived from those same products and services. In some cases, they are in fact making it more difficult for their own firms to manage the sale and delivery of these "added value" products and services.

Take word processing equipment as an example. Forty years ago, an administrative manager who was shopping for word processing power chose between a manual typewriter and an electric model, perhaps the classic IBM Selectric. Typewriters differed in price and features, but the choice was fairly straightforward.

Thirty years ago, the manager's choices expanded to include dedicated word processors. This choice was still relatively uncomplicated, but it marked the beginning of a value gap between expectations and outcomes. The product performed, but it also drove the need for additional training and skill development within the administrative staff and opened the opportunity for more complex shared word processing centers—many of which later failed. Cost-effective word processing, nevertheless, was still the sole criterion for the purchaser.

Twenty years ago, the manager's choice became exponentially more complex with the widespread adoption of multifunctional personal computers. These machines processed words and ran financial spreadsheets. They came in a seemingly infinite number of configurations, and they required significant employee training, software, and printers as well as a technical staff to support and maintain the system. It was becoming more difficult to evaluate and implement word processing solutions.

Ten years ago, the personal computer had almost wholly eliminated the venerable typewriter, but the complexity of the buyer's decision and implementation challenges continued to multiply as networks and the Internet emerged. The manager had to consider the loss of centralized control that these machines represented, the security of the network, LAN integration, and so forth. In fact, the manager was no longer qualified or solely responsible for this purchase. IT and functional managers throughout the company were involved and often became the primary decision makers for the new systems.

Today, with some exceptions, word processing itself has disappeared as a dedicated function. If still working after 40-odd years, our manager must now be aware of many issues, including security (viruses in macros), collaboration, document and file management, document analysis and classification, file format integrity, and site licenses, to name just a few.[2]

Throughout the past 40 years, sellers have focused on adding value at each level of word processing development. In doing so, word processing has become a ubiquitous function available to almost every employee in and out of the office. But again, inherent in that added value is added complexity. Additional complexity negatively impacts the realization of value, because value achievement depends on more than the product or service itself. Value achievement is also contingent on the quality of the decision process used to make the purchase and the successful implementation and use of the solution—both of which become more difficult as complexity increases.

It is useful to approach the complexity challenge associated with business-to-business solutions in terms of three eras of evolutionary change. John Sullivan, a colleague with a Ph.D. in instructional design, first described them in a survey of a half-century of sales training for a course he developed and taught at the University of Minnesota. The three eras, which span the business environment from 1950 to the current day, offer an accessible, accurate means of understanding today's paradoxical situation, in which the expansion of the value promise by the seller can dilute value achievement for the buyer.

ERA ONE
Obvious Value

In the 1950s, sellers in the business-to-business sector created a product and sent it off to markets filled with the "hungry" consumers of the post–WWII era. Prospective customers were shown the product and decided whether or not it made sense to buy it. They either signed a deal or said no.

This sounds overly simple, but it is a generally accurate reflection of that time. The business-to-business world worked on the premise that if a company created a product that customers truly wanted, it need only notify them of its availability. The customer would clearly see the value and write a check.

Let's revisit Peter Drucker. He precisely reflected the thinking of this period when, in 1954, he identified innovation and marketing as the only two functions of a business. The marketing function determined what the customer needed. The innovation function created it, and then marketing presented it to the customer. Twenty years later, Drucker could still write:

> There will always, one can assume, be need for some selling. But the aim of marketing is to make selling superfluous. The aim of marketing is to know and understand the customer so well that the product and service fits him and sells itself.
>
> Ideally, marketing should result in a customer who is ready to buy. All that should be needed then is to make the product or service available; i.e., logistics rather than salesmanship, and statistical distribution rather than promotion.[3]

As I write this, I can't help but think this could be the epicenter of the animosity we so often see between sales and marketing. The idealistic assumption behind the idea that a product or service can "sell itself" is that customers can clearly comprehend the offering and evaluate its value in light of their own circumstances. Indeed, in Era One, which Sullivan identified as spanning the period between 1950 and the mid-1970s, that was generally the case. Products, for the most part, hadn't yet developed into complex solutions and the customer was able to understand the problems to be solved. Value tended to be inherent in the features of the product, and the value or "benefits" of the features was readily apparent to the buyer.

Drucker *was* preaching a radical change when he suggested that the customer's agenda should be the central focus of business. The typical company of that day was still creating the products and services it wanted and was using its sales force to push them on customers. In Era One, the seller's agenda, which was to persuade customers to do what it wanted them to do, dominated the marketplace. Salespeople were seen as *persuaders*. Their training focused almost exclusively on presentation, closing, and the manipulation of the customer. Their skills were grounded in stimulus-response and compliance theories.[4]

This wasn't an ideal situation in terms of customer relationships, but in terms of value achievement, it wasn't a critical problem, either. In Era One, buyers easily understood their own problems and the seller's products. They could achieve value on their own, and they willingly accepted responsibility for achieving that value.

ERA TWO
Augmented Value

In Era Two, a period Sullivan identifies as extending for an approximately 20-year period from the mid-1970s to the mid-1990s, business-to-business transactions became more sophisticated. This sophistication was embodied in a changing view of the value inherent in products and services and how that value should be presented and delivered to customers.

Theodore Levitt, the marketing guru from Harvard Business School, articulated and influenced the widespread acceptance of the changes that took place during Era Two. Levitt started from the customercentric value platform that Drucker espoused, then suggested that businesses should add new levels of value in the quest for competitive advantage through differentiation.

Products had a "range of possibilities," according to Levitt. There was the *generic product*—the thing itself without any added value; the *expected product*—whose added value was limited to the minimal expectations of the customer; the *augmented product*—

to which the seller added value beyond the customer's basic wants and raised the bar for competition; and the *potential product*—which encompassed all of the value possibilities that could be imagined.[5]

Levitt's augmented product concept was the foundation for today's "whole" solutions, and sellers began to compete with this new strategy. They added value by direct product improvement *and* by enhancing the bundle of services and other intangibles that accompanied their products. In doing so, they moved the business-to-business sector into Era Two.

For example, in Era One, an escalator provided a clear value—the transport of people between levels. Its characteristics—the price, the precision of the parts, its appearance, etc.—were inherent in the product itself. In Era Two, the product that is an escalator became something more. It may have included, among other things, a financing scheme, an installation plan, and a service and support agreement—each of which had to be understood, evaluated, and implemented. Value may also have been added in the product itself (perhaps the escalator was now controlled by a computer), making its implementation and operation more difficult. Thus, the decision to buy and the achievement of value became more problematic.

Levitt heralded the transition to Era Two, but he also astutely recognized its ramifications as they applied to the achievement of customer value. In 1975, in his comments on the republication of his famous *Harvard Business Review* article "Marketing Myopia" (1960), he wrote:

> Companies have attempted to "serve" customers by creating complex and beautifully efficient products or services that buyers are too risk-averse to adopt or incapable of learning how to employ—in effect, there are now steam shovels for people who haven't yet learned to use spades.[6]

Sellers responded by revamping their marketing and sales efforts to reflect the customer's need for assistance. The consultative approach to sales emerged, emphasizing questioning, listening, and building trust. The salesperson acted as a *problem solver,* whose job was to get customers to confide their problems and then match them to the selling company's solutions.

In Era Two, buyers could still understand their own problems, but they needed help to understand the augmented products being offered. They needed sellers to explain and possibly install and start up the solution to capture its value.

ERA THREE
Complex Value Networks

Enter Era Three, a period that Sullivan identifies as emerging in the mid-1990s. The business-to-business sector moved into Era Three when the speed of change and the complexity of problems began to expand beyond the buyer's easy comprehension. Additionally, other forces such as environmental, workplace, and safety regulations began to play a critical part in changing products and systems, making decisions far more complex and difficult.

Technological advances created much of this change. The Internet is one obvious example. The technology enabling the integration and networking of business systems is another. Certainly, business-to-business buyers are still struggling with the exponential increase in choices brought about by these developments.

Complex developments make it more difficult for buyers to understand their own situations, needs, and problems. They may know what their ultimate goals are (e.g., "We want a real-time scorecard for all our businesses available to the leadership team.") without clearly understanding which components are most important and how existing systems impose unique constraints.

Concurrently, sellers are using the same technological advances to develop ever more complex and expensive solutions, such as the new RFID (radio-frequency identification) inventory tracking systems already mandated by Wal-mart and the Department of Defense, with which their customers have no previous experience. Thus, Levitt's Era Two warning is still a relevant issue.

Harvard Business School's Clayton Christensen confirms that in Era Three, solution sellers continue to outrun the comprehension and requirements of customers. He calls the phenomena "performance oversupply."[7] This ensures that the Era Two dilemma, of not understanding the solution, continues to deepen.

No wonder, then, that customers in Era Three have difficulty understanding their problems, the proposed solutions, and the solution implementation process. Under these conditions, how can they be expected to choose, implement, and successfully achieve the value from "best" offerings? They cannot.

Most business-to-business buying teams are not equipped to make a high-quality decision in each of the complex situations they face. In October 2003, in a Microsoft Office Live Meeting "webinar," over 400 solution providers were polled to see if they believed their customers had high-quality decision processes in place. They were also asked if those customers were capable of evaluating both the depth of their problems and the technologies and solutions the providers offered. Of those complex solution providers who responded, 78 percent said no.[8]

The group was also asked to rank their customers' level of knowledge regarding their problems and the solution alternatives available. This time, the majority of the respondents (78 percent) ranked their customers' at 60 percent or below.

The same levels of difficulty extend to solution implementation, helping to explain why solution failure rates are high.

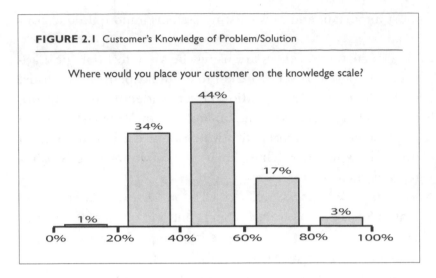

FIGURE 2.1 Customer's Knowledge of Problem/Solution

It doesn't take a leap of logic to conclude that, if customers cannot make the best solution decisions and effectively implement them, there is little hope that they will achieve the value promised.

To exacerbate the entire situation further, corporate downsizing results in fewer managers per worker, higher employee turnover rates, and lower experience levels per employee. How have buyers responded to this dilemma? Clearly, companies have low expectations of receiving help from vendors. Many companies have formed teams to buy products and services, hoping that the added input from the different functions will better define the problem and solution. Others have increased the size and skills of their purchasing departments. Frequently, however, these efforts continue to commoditize offerings, often pushing sellers further away. The opportunity for a truly collaborative solution development, which is required in this new environment, is further subverted.

In short, in Era Three, value complexity is the primary feature of the business-to-business landscape. Customers need more help than ever in diagnosing their problems *and* in designing, evaluating, and implementing solutions and achieving the complex, customized, and unique value they promise. But where are the sellers?

I must clarify that the characteristics of an Era Three organization are by no means unique to the 21st century. A small percentage of top performing organizations have marketed, sold, and delivered Prime Solutions throughout the 1900s. No doubt we could venture further back in time and find notable examples as well. As we think of major innovations, by definition, if companies had not provided a Prime Solution, acceptance of the innovation might never have occurred. To cite just a few examples, the first computers sold by IBM, the first cash registers sold by NCR, and the first fax machines sold by Western Union all required a unique knowledge of the customer's business and the ability to support the customer as they implemented the many changes required by the new technology. The Prime Solution is not unique to the 21st century, but it is very quickly becoming the price of admission.

IN WHAT ERA ARE YOU POSITIONED?

By and large, sellers have not recognized the shift into Era Three and the dilemma this shift has caused for their customers, nor have they adjusted their business processes to reflect it. Most companies are developing, marketing, selling, and supporting Levitt's augmented products as if they are still positioned in Era Two.

The most obvious manifestation of Era Two thinking can be seen in the overwhelming emphasis that sellers place on solution features and benefits. Today's marketing focus and the resulting sales collateral and messaging tend to be about the capabilities of the solutions themselves—or the rosy future a customer who acquires the solution is sure to experience. The customer is left to connect the dots.

Sales presentations and proposals are a quick and simple way to gauge in which era a seller is operating. Examine your company's typical sales presentation and/or proposal. If you are operating in Era Two, it will probably be inward looking, focused on you, your company, your solution and its benefits, and the future you can deliver for the customer.

When the solution providers at the webinar were asked to characterize the content of their own presentations and proposals, three-quarters of the group responded that 70 percent or more of their content was focused on their own companies, their solutions, and the future results they would bring the customer. Only 9 percent said that their proposals and presentations gave nearly equal time (between 40 percent and 60 percent) to the problem and the customer's world. The underlying assumption behind seller-focused presentations and proposals is the misguided belief that the customer has a very high comprehension level and understands its own problem. Further, an equally misguided belief is that when the customer sees your solution, it will recognize its value, will easily be able to differentiate the value of the competitive offerings, and, in essence, is fully capable of making an informed, quality decision.

Another obvious manifestation of Era Two thinking can be found in the seller's postsale processes. What does your company's postsale involvement look like? If it is in Era Two, the actual sale or, possibly, the successful installation of the solution tends to conclude the transaction. Levitt succinctly summed this up when he wrote:

The seller has made a sale, which he expects directly to yield a profit (to the seller's company). The buyer has bought a tool with which to produce things to make a profit. For the seller it is the end of the process; for the buyer the beginning.[9]

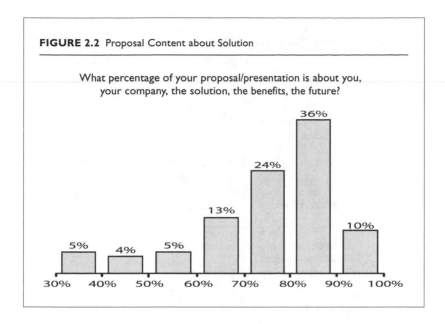

FIGURE 2.2 Proposal Content about Solution

What percentage of your proposal/presentation is about you, your company, the solution, the benefits, the future?

Postinstallation activities for Era Two sellers are typically relegated to servicing defective products or providing updates and support via a maintenance contract. This can be summed up as: "We installed it; it's working; give us a call if it breaks." The era in which sellers are operating becomes dishearteningly clear when their response to a solution failure is a shrug and a flip remark, "They [the customer] didn't do it right."

Interestingly, sellers usually recognize that they aren't operating in Era Three. When the 400 solution providers in the Microsoft Office Live Meeting webinar were asked in which era they would place the majority of their colleagues, the answers were not surprising. Eighty-four percent responded that their colleagues were operating in either Era One or Era Two.

This gets us to an important cause of the solution failure epidemic and the expansion of the Value Gap. Most sellers are utilizing Era Two systems and processes to assist customers who are struggling to achieve value in complex businesses—businesses clearly situated in Era Three. As a result, sellers are not properly structured or equipped to support the customers'

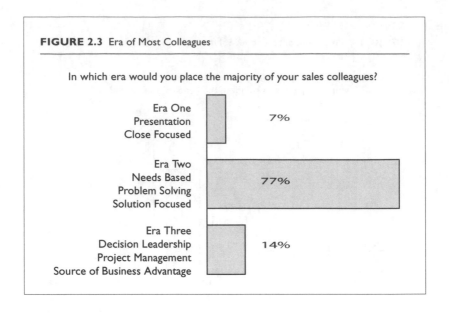

FIGURE 2.3 Era of Most Colleagues

In which era would you place the majority of your sales colleagues?

Era One
Presentation
Close Focused — 7%

Era Two
Needs Based
Problem Solving
Solution Focused — 77%

Era Three
Decision Leadership
Project Management
Source of Business Advantage — 14%

requirements. They are focused on *selling* the existing solution rather than *creating* a solution that would produce the customer's desired outcomes. Worse, sellers' and buyers' interests tend to be misaligned, and they end up working at cross-purposes.

BUSINESS ADVANTAGE IN ERA THREE

In Era One, business-to-business sellers were persuaders. In Era Two, they became problem solvers. In Era Three, they must become *sources of business advantage* for their customers.

For instance, a solution provider who embraces this approach would seek out a substantially greater degree of involvement in the diagnosis of the customer's situation and its relationship to the offered solution, whereas in an earlier era, a solution provider would expect a customer to undertake this task as easily as they would a simple math equation. An Era Three professional would understand that the customer might well have neither the time nor the expertise to conduct an evaluation of exponential complexity.

As we discussed above, one place that this expectation would manifest itself would be in the vendor's presentations and proposals. Era Three customers need as much help understanding the extent and cost of their problems as they do understanding your solutions. Thus, we would expect to see approximately half of a presentation or proposal focused on clarifying the customer's situation, their business challenges, and their objectives.

A company that positions itself in the "source of business advantage" role would also behave very differently in the post-sale period. In previous years, a seller could "drop it at the dock" or install the product and then move on. In Era Three, however, the focus changes from, "It's functioning," to, "You are getting the value we promised." This paradigm shift is very significant. When the seller commits to the customer's value achievement, it adopts an extended vision of value accountability. With this mentality, you and your company will be operating squarely in Era Three.

An additional, very important focus in Era Three, as we move to monitoring ongoing customer value achievement, is, "What other value creation opportunities can we discover in this collaborative relationship?"

One way that this change would manifest is through offering a higher level and broader range of postsale services. This isn't necessarily a harbinger of higher costs. These may very well be services that your customer would be happy to pay for and would generate a new source of profit for your business.

That is exactly what CEO and Dell Computer founder Michael Dell has discovered. In early 2004, he announced that the perennially successful direct marketer's revenues from product support and warranty services were growing twice as fast as any other part of the company.[10] The growth of outsourcing is also evidence of the value of, and customer demand for, postsale services. Providers of outsourced services can be seen as the ultimate manifestation of the Era Three solution provider. Their business model could be summarized as: "We are so concerned that you get the full value of our solution, that we will do it for you."

For the seller, the shift to Era Three is not a simple one, especially when problem and solution complexity continue to increase exponentially. Transforming into a source of business advantage for customers is a tall order. It requires your company to work hard at getting beyond the limiting construct of value promises and into a new world in which you ensure sustainable value achievement.

This can't be accomplished without collaboration among key functions within your own organization as well as the customer's organization. To become a source of business advantage, we must first identify and discover the value opportunity. Sales, marketing, R&D, and customer support must all recognize their role in keeping a vigilant watch for new value creation opportunities. When these are identified, marketing must profile potential markets for the potential solution and create the value messaging and diagnostic strategy. R&D must design and create a solution that is value capable. Service and support must be ready to assist in the successful implementation of your solution *and* the ongoing measurement of results. Sales completes the cycle by ensuring that customers clearly understand the absence of value and that your solution is the right answer to their business problems.

Focusing on the customer's achievement of value and engaging in a high level of participation is a distinctly different role than Levitt described. No longer should your process end and the customer's begin at the point of sale. Instead, there is a collaborative process of value release in Era Three. Your processes, along with your customer's processes, are expanded and merged, until both encompass the whole cycle and chain of events in the creation, exchange, and achievement of value. This merging of processes is described in greater detail throughout this book.

Becoming a source of business advantage to your customer in Era Three and ensuring that advantage is achieved and sustained represents the most substantial opportunity for differentiation and competitive advantage in today's business-to-business marketplace. Customers are hungry for—if not demanding—outright answers to their Era Three dilemmas. Stated more strongly, companies that do not move to Era Three selling will be left behind, as customers become more openly frustrated with undelivered promises of value. Based on the evidence we've seen in the marketplace, a surprisingly low number of businesses are currently positioned to consistently meet those demands.

There are real barriers for a company to move to Era Three. One such barrier is a dependence on outmoded processes and techniques. Others are the defense mechanisms that buyers have adopted to protect themselves from the residual effects of the Era One and Era Two sellers and current methodologies that continue to reflect these bygone eras. These barriers need to be defined and addressed before the Value Gap can be closed.

3

FIVE BARRIERS TO KEEPING VALUE PROMISES

One way to understand the misalignment between buyers and sellers in business-to-business marketplaces is to look at plate tectonics. We can visualize the Value Gap as a major fault line running between the two massive plates of Era Two and Era Three. Like the spaces between the earth's plates, the break is neither clean nor easily closed.

The pressure that builds as the earth's plates grind against each other is enormous, and it creates jagged outcroppings, deep fissures, and constant earthquakes. Similar barriers have arisen around the fault line in the business-to-business sector. These barriers act as obstacles to both buyers and sellers in the quest for value achievement. As a result, unless the solution and the seller are equipped to overcome the barriers, the buyer will have a difficult time achieving the promised value.

Five barriers must be addressed by a Prime Solution seller. They are:

1. *Relevancy Barrier.* Sellers unilaterally define the solution and, thus, are unable to create value that is meaningful to customers.
2. *Inflation Barrier.* Sellers focus on benefits and features, sidestepping their duty to inform customers of the hurdles and risks to value achievement.
3. *Comprehension Barrier.* Sellers incorrectly assume that customers are capable of understanding their own complex problems and the complex solutions.
4. *Dilution Barrier.* Sellers accept the widely used, price-based commodity approach to buying decisions and allow customers to unknowingly strip the value out of their solutions.
5. *Implementation Barrier.* Sellers avoid value accountability and blame customers for solution failures.

Let's take a closer look at each of the barriers and their consequences in business-to-business solution selling.

THE RELEVANCY BARRIER

Customers are the ultimate judges of value. If they perceive value in a solution, they make the investment. If not, they don't. This is a basic tenet of economics, yet the first and most fundamental barrier between companies and their customers arises around the issue of value definition.

In today's markets for complex solutions, one would assume that value definition is always a customercentric process. But noncustomer-centered definitions of value are more the rule than the exception.

Several years ago, our firm was asked to analyze a solution that was not generating anticipated sales. The solution was a recording system for police interrogations and other interviews governed by strict legal guidelines. It was designed to create a legally unassailable and continuous record of a conversation with time and voice stamps. Such a record would help eliminate the judicial suppression of confessions on technical grounds, a common problem in law enforcement.

When the recorder was released, most of the major urban police departments bought a single unit for testing, and all agreed that it worked exactly as promised. But multiple unit orders never materialized. What went wrong?

There turned out to be an insurmountable problem in value relevancy. On the one hand, the company was right: police departments didn't want confessions suppressed, and they would buy a solution for that problem. On the other hand, the company did not realize that law enforcement officials *do not* want the entire interrogation process, along with every strategy and tactic used to elicit a confession, recorded and handed to defense attorneys and their clients.

The seller had uncovered all the reasons why customers in the target market *would* buy the product but ignored all the reasons why they *wouldn't*. Value was improperly defined, and the solution ended up creating a problem that was bigger than the one it solved. The potential customer's pain of change was greater than the pain of remaining the same. The recorder was scrapped, and a $4 million investment and two years of work were lost.

A loss of a few million dollars would be a painful but ultimately absorbable cost for most major companies, but occasionally a collision with the Relevancy Barrier can bury an entire company. When Iridium LLC, for example, ran into the barrier in 1999, the result was corporate bankruptcy.

Iridium was founded on a breakthrough idea that had surfaced at Motorola in the late 1980s. The vision was to create the

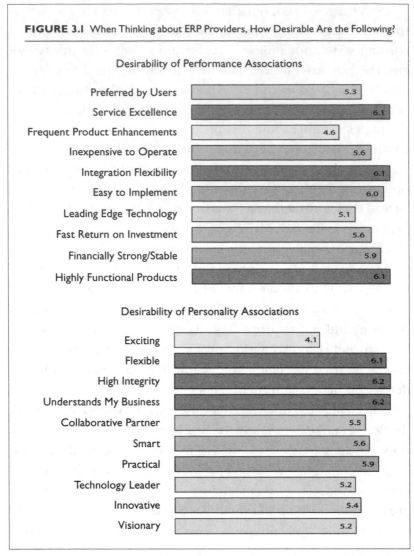

FIGURE 3.1 When Thinking about ERP Providers, How Desirable Are the Following?

Desirability of Performance Associations

Preferred by Users	5.3
Service Excellence	6.1
Frequent Product Enhancements	4.6
Inexpensive to Operate	5.6
Integration Flexibility	6.1
Easy to Implement	6.0
Leading Edge Technology	5.1
Fast Return on Investment	5.6
Financially Strong/Stable	5.9
Highly Functional Products	6.1

Desirability of Personality Associations

Exciting	4.1
Flexible	6.1
High Integrity	6.2
Understands My Business	6.2
Collaborative Partner	5.5
Smart	5.6
Practical	5.9
Technology Leader	5.2
Innovative	5.4
Visionary	5.2

Reprinted with permission of The Yankee Group, http://www.yankeegroup.com.

first global wireless telephone network, a network enabled by a complex grid of 66 satellites orbiting 420 miles above the earth. Toward that end, Motorola formed Iridium, a consortium of aerospace and communications companies that built and launched the network and created service deals in countries around the world.

In 1998, within a few months of its targeted completion date, Iridium opened for business and launched wireless phone service available anywhere on the planet. There was, however, one major problem. In 1987, cell phones had been rare, and Iridium's definition of value was robust. By 1998, over a half-billion people around the world owned cell phones, and the value of Iridium's solution had shrunk until there was not enough demand left to support the business. In the year 2000, the bankrupt company was sold for a half-penny on the dollar—$25 million for a $5 billion investment.[1]

The above examples may give the impression that only individual companies crash up against the Relevancy Barrier. The truth is that entire industries get involved in multicompany pile-ups.

Witness the results of an Enterprise Resource Planning systems (ERP) *BrandMonitor* survey conducted by The Yankee Group and released in January 2004. The survey found that ERP brand loyalty among business decision makers was very weak and that buyers perceived only "muted" differences between the major vendors. More disturbingly, it also uncovered a significant disconnect in how value is defined in the ERP marketplace.

Here's how Yankee Group program manager Jon Derome interpreted the responses.

> Vendors promote speeds, feeds, and technology prowess, but, according to our respondents, these traits are not meaningful or relevant to the basic challenges ERP customers face today. Decision makers tell us that they want service, flexibility, and practicality. Unfortunately, none of the major brands differentiates itself along these lines, leaving the door wide open for any one of the category providers to address these unmet needs.[2]

This is a direct reflection of a decades-old problem. Companies continue to define value based on their own perceptions of the marketplace. In high-technology industries, these perceptions are usually driven by an internal desire for ever more sophisticated, elegant products and services or by the actions of competitors, who are driven by the same desires. Thus, value capability—what the solution can do—becomes the central issue in product and service development.

The primary effect of industrywide pile-ups at the Relevancy Barrier is that solution sellers alienate buyers. This situation may be neither immediately apparent nor fatal. As long as everyone else is also alienating buyers, as The Yankee Group found in the ERP solutions marketplace, the customer does not have much choice except to pick among limited alternatives.

But what happens when an existing seller or, more likely, a newcomer with a fresh perspective, gets wise to Derome's final thought and decides to fulfill the unmet needs of buyers? Then a new leader appears, and everyone else has to scramble to maintain market share.

What ERP solution sellers and many others are ignoring is the reality that, when they unilaterally define products and services, they may well create solutions with limited value to customers. The customer's requirements for value achievement, not the technological capability of the product or service itself, must be the driving consideration in solution development.

THE INFLATION BARRIER

The business-to-business seller's focus has traditionally been features and benefits. Typically, an Era Two solution seller will meet with prospective customers and launch into "The Presentation"—a tenured and time-honored element of the sales process. Presentations are almost always intensely focused on the characteristics of the solution and the glowing future of any company that is smart enough to purchase it. The problem is that, with every new explicit and implicit promise, the seller is by omission and, often, by commission raising the Inflation Barrier.

The presentation of features and benefits is actually an indirect cause of the barrier. It is not what sellers are doing that causes the barrier; it is what they are *not* doing. When they are talking about features and benefits, they are *not* learning about the unique circumstances present in the customer's business— circumstances that always impact the success of the solution and return on investment. Equally important, they are also *not* discussing the operational and cultural changes the customer must undertake to implement the solution successfully.

These same elements, when ignored, are primary contributors to solution failures. When their impact is not quantified, the total cost of the solution cannot be accurately calculated, and the situation deteriorates even further. The cost is invariably underestimated. As a result, the value the customer places on the solution can be inflated beyond achievable levels.

A glaring example can be seen in the myriad solutions associated with sales force automation (SFA). SFA solutions have had a series of head-on collisions with the Inflation Barrier over the past decade.

The value in SFA has always been readily apparent. It enables the business to push and pull critical information to and from the front lines of their customer interactions. Catalogs, product specifications, technical support, real-time inventory, and any other information a salesperson might conceivably need can be accessed via a laptop computer and carried into the customer's office. Customer orders, requests, and problems can be delivered back to the proper place within the organization in seconds. When salespeople diligently enter critical data, SFA provides a convenient tool for managing their own productivity and gives executives a means of managing and enhancing that productivity.

History repeated itself when it came to solution success rates. A Gartner Group, Inc. survey found that, "At least 60 percent of sales force automation projects fail to produce measurable benefits, and more than 75 percent of the businesses that install such systems are dissatisfied."[3]

Two of the most common problems have nothing to do with the features and benefits of the solutions. First is the customer's sales process itself. SFA cannot deliver the promised benefits if the customer has a nonexistent or dysfunctional sales process, which is frequently the case. Second, the success of SFA is directly related to the training and cooperation of the sales force. Unfortunately, many organizations skipped the training. Further, they did not take into account the high resistance of salespeople to a solution that sometimes looked more like a big stick.

The Inflation Barrier proved to be a formidable obstacle in SFA, because many solution sellers did not inform customers of these critical issues. Instead, they demonstrated and sold the impressive capabilities of their software. In turn, their frustrated customers responded to the ensuing solution failures by trying to find better solutions. In 2001, Erin Kinikin, an analyst at Giga Information, told *ComputerWorld* that most of the SFA customers she worked with were "on their second or third vendor—and looking for another. [This] spending in *Fortune* 5,000 companies [and in opportunity-driven industries] runs into millions of dollars per company, without showing clear results."[4]

Sellers reinforce the Inflation Barrier in two ways. The first is through the error of omission: sellers studiously avoid divulging any information that may negatively influence the buyer. The error is driven by fear—the seller is afraid of losing the sale. We often see salespeople make this error, which is also prevalent among solution developers and marketers. This erroneous sales behavior can result from a lack of direction, the "you're on your own" school of management.

The second error—the error of commission—is even more serious, because it represents the institutionalization of the first error. In this case, the entire workforce is taught a very narrow definition of solution functionality and encouraged to ignore the broader implications of their solutions. In such a company, the sales force is instructed that its sole job is to present features, benefits, and competitive superiority. They learn that issues surrounding the solution, namely the customer's unique circumstances and implementation considerations, are "not our concern." They are, in effect, commissioned to omit critical information, thereby frequently undermining the business relationship.

THE COMPREHENSION BARRIER

One often-heard response to solution failures is that the customer should have known better. However, given the complexity of problems and solutions characteristic of Era Three, customers *do not* know better. Furthermore, most sellers *do not* realize how much their customers do not know. This is the root cause of the Comprehension Barrier.

Most sellers of complex products and services are bombarding their customers with painstakingly prepared presentations, but their customers comprehend only one-quarter of what's being said.

This information usually comes as a shock to solution sellers, but that figure is based on their own estimates. A buyer's comprehension can be measured using two scales: one represents the level of customers' knowledge of the problem and solution alternatives, and the other represents their progression through the decision process. When we ask professional salespeople where their customers tend to fall on the two scales, then plot the customers on a Decision Challenge graph, roughly three-quarters of the graph's field remains uncovered. That uncovered portion is the information outside the customer's area of comprehension.[5]

This comprehension percentage can drop even lower in newly developed markets. The early adopters in new solution markets often experience higher failure rates than those who buy later, a logical consequence of inexperience. As a solution market becomes more established, the knowledge base grows. Thus, comprehension levels tend to rise over time.

As this book is being written, radio frequency identification (RFID) is emerging as a major new solution market. RFID tags and readers enable retailers, for example, to process and track individual products from the vendor, to the distribution warehouse, to store shelves, into customer hands, and beyond. When that level and immediacy of information is integrated with enterprise-level systems, RFID holds the potential to change radically the way business is conducted.

Retailing giant Wal-Mart jump-started the RFID market, when it announced that its 100 largest suppliers must add RFID tags to all of their products by January 2005. Also, the Department of Defense has asked its suppliers to place RFID tags on pallet-size deliveries by that same date.

The opportunity of RFID is clear, but the buyers of these solutions are nevertheless faced with many questions. To date, only a few pilot programs have been run, and standards are still being defined. Knowledge regarding how to achieve the value inherent in RFID is very low. Here's how Sun Microsystems product line manager Vijay Sarathy described the situation to *Inside 1to1* in early 2004: "There's managing data, security, provisioning data—making sure the right data syncs to the backend system—no one understands it."[6]

If past results indicate future performance, we can expect that companies in this market will overestimate the knowledge levels of their customers, and a collision with the Comprehension Barrier may well be inevitable. It is a good bet that RFID failures will be making headlines over the next several years.

THE DILUTION BARRIER

One of the great ironies of the current business-to-business environment is that, while buyers are ravenous for value-laden solutions, the systems and processes that they have in place to purchase products and services strip the value out of the solution before it can be delivered. This is the Dilution Barrier—and companies run headlong into it every day.

Companies hit the Dilution Barrier when they allow their solutions to be treated like commodities, then compete on price. When buyers, notably the purchasing department, insist on treating complex solutions as commodities, sellers often comply by splitting their solutions into components and selling the pieces. The pieces, however, do not deliver the value inherent in the complete solution.

The Dilution Barrier is reinforced in several ways. One is the standard price-based or commodity approach to purchasing that is in place at so many companies. A commodity-based approach to buying complex solutions is driven mainly by purchasing departments, whose mandate is often to lower the acquisition cost. Unfortunately, the purchasing department is usually *not* held accountable for the value a solution delivers in business performance terms. In their quest to save dollars of cost, frequently more dollars of value are lost—a blatant example of crossfunctional dysfunction. All too often, the purchasing department is allowed, and even encouraged, to exclude value from their acquisition process.

Purchasing departments are not the only culprits. The complexity of problems and solutions and the lack of comprehension endemic within the marketplace are also significant supporting factors in the Dilution Barrier. As we saw in the Comprehension Barrier, even customers who will be working with solutions often have a difficult time understanding the ramifications of value. When customers do not understand the parameters of their problems and the capabilities of the solution alternatives, they cannot quantify value. Price, the lowest common denominator, naturally becomes the primary factor in the buying decision.

To deal with complexity, customers also attempt to create simplistic standards of comparison. Thus, they will demand that sellers strip components out of their solutions to achieve the infamous apples-to-apples comparison. Sellers who are under pressure to make sales often allow this arbitrary dilution of value to occur. The result is reduced competitive differentiation, lower margins, and ultimately, solutions that cannot deliver on their full value potential.

The barrier gets reinforced once more when a seller fails to field an effective defense against the customer's commoditization effort. The sad reality is that most solution providers follow a selling process that virtually guarantees that they will have to make price concessions to make the sale. When they cannot ensure that the customer can quantify the financial impact of this dilution of value, the value of the complete potential solution remains unrealized. To be sure, there is a challenge on the "initial sale" to recognize and credit "potential" or "promised" value prior to its actual delivery.

Oddly, value dilution often corresponds with a seller's own shortsighted behaviors. Pricing solutions on cost rather than value is one such pitfall. One study found that 70 percent of the manufacturing companies surveyed relied on the traditional cost-plus model to set their prices.[7]

Further, many sellers are determining their own purchases of complex products and services based on price alone. When they buy the components that will go into their solutions based on price, they strip value from the end product. By treating their vendor's product and services as commodities, they literally impose limitations on value that is then built into their solutions.

This all eventually trickles down to the customer. If sellers are not pricing their solutions based on value and are not buying the components that the solutions are built around based on value, it is hard to argue that customers should take a more enlightened, value-based approach to purchasing.

The main consequence of these behaviors is a collision with the Dilution Barrier. Sellers do survive the crash, but their solutions emerge on the other side stripped of their value. And stunted value capability obviously yields stunted value achievement.

THE IMPLEMENTATION BARRIER

One experience most of us have in common is that of buying a product, bringing it home, and not being able to get it to work properly. Perhaps you don't have all of the equipment you need to make it work—a splitter cable to hook that new DVD recorder-player into your home theater, for instance. Or maybe you lack the expertise needed to install and use the product—such as not being able to get that new version of the operating system software to work on your personal computer. Multiply the frustration and anger you feel when that happens by a thousand, and you get a sense of what it feels like to hit the Implementation Barrier.

Business-to-business buyers collide with the Implementation Barrier when they cannot get solutions working properly. The solution may be inherently flawed, but much more often conditions within the buyer's organization cause this barrier.

In some cases, they simply do not have the internal expertise required to install the solution. This shouldn't come as much of surprise after what we learned earlier about buyer comprehension levels pertaining to complex solutions and the examples of ERP implementation failures described in Chapter 1.

In other cases, a collision with an Implementation Barrier is triggered after the solution is successfully installed, because the buyer is not capable of using it properly. Years ago, our firm worked with a client who had created one of the first automated statistical process control (SPC) solutions. Manufacturers bought the solution; they realized that SPC was an important key to high-quality output. The solution was successfully installed and produced large volumes of data, but no one was exactly sure what the data meant or how it should be used to improve process results. Predictably, sales were quickly and negatively impacted.

Solution sellers reinforce the Implementation Barrier when they narrowly define their accountability for their customer's value achievement. Sometimes, as was prevalent in Era One, they merely deliver the solution and leave the buyer to struggle with installation. Or more commonly, in behavior characteristic of Era Two, they do install the solution but leave the buyer to achieve the value. Both scenarios are common and lead to collisions with the Implementation Barrier.

A narrow definition of value accountability can also exacerbate the result of an Implementation Barrier crash. Customers will naturally look to sellers for redress after a solution failure. Sellers will respond as if they have delivered everything the customer is entitled to and deny responsibility. The blame game now begins with all of the usual consequences.

The odd thing about sellers who react like this is that they are very often missing a lucrative opportunity to build market share and profits. The seller of SPC solutions described above responded to the Implementation Barrier by creating and offering support systems, including SPC training seminars, materials, and books. The company quickly became the market leader.

THREE CONSIDERATIONS FOR BRINGING DOWN THE BARRIERS

In the process of examining the five barriers, three considerations emerge that lead us to believe that the barriers must be treated as a monolithic set of obstacles.

First, while it is critical to understand the causes of the barriers, the purpose of that understanding is not to assign blame. The *seller* is identified as the guilty party in the definition of each barrier, because the seller must overcome the barriers to create a successful sale and a strong relationship with the buyer.

In reality, buyers are sometimes the catalyst behind a barrier. For instance, prospective customers who insist on evaluating solution alternatives based on price alone are guilty of stripping the value out of a transaction, and this may well create a barrier that sellers must struggle to overcome. This struggle, by the way, is not simply about making a sale (you can reduce the price and write the business at a lower margin); it is about ensuring the customer's value achievement.

When buyers behave in ways that appear to be contrary to their own self-interest, sellers need to uncover and address the reasons. When buyers insist on approaching a transaction as a cost-based decision, it may be that they simply do not understand the differences between unique solutions. Or, often, they believe that they must protect themselves from manipulation by sellers. In the case of the procurement function, they may be acting according to a legacy culture or a set of incentives inconsistent with those of the overall firm. Overcoming such barriers will be addressed in detail later in Chapter 5, "Multiple Decisions, Mutual Understandings."

The best way to approach the barriers is to understand that, no matter whether they are buyer driven or seller driven, sellers who do not understand and address them will be forced either to walk away empty-handed or make concessions that limit the buyer's value. In the former case, the revenue from the transaction and potential of the relationship slips away altogether. In the latter, the margins are reduced and, ultimately, the seller's market position is negatively impacted. Again, this is why the barriers are framed in terms of sellers—sellers must address them to succeed in the complex solutions marketplace.

Second, one barrier often supports and reinforces another. Picture this common scenario: a salesperson is struggling to overcome the objections of a customer who is fixated on a solution's price tag. In a misguided effort to write new business, the salesperson inflates the ROI by aggressively pitching the value promise and glossing over the challenges and risks inherent in a successful implementation. The customer buys, but when it comes time to implement the solution, is not prepared to deal with the unexpected, and a solution failure starts to unfold. Thus the Dilution Barrier leads to the Inflation Barrier, which, in turn, leads to the Implementation Barrier.

Because the barriers tend to be interrelated and reinforcing, sellers need to be prepared to recognize and address all five. Further, as they create strategies to overcome one barrier, sellers must also ensure that the consequences of those strategies do not turn other barriers into insurmountable obstacles.

Third, the point at which the consequences of a barrier manifest is often not *where the collision actually takes place.* For instance, when the value definition of a solution is flawed, the consequences may not appear until the sales force discovers that customers will not buy the solution. Sellers tend to assume mistakenly that the cause of the problem is sales related. They try to solve it at that point, often causing to greater damage.

Granted, the consequences of the barriers tend to appear toward the end of the value process, because that is where the rubber hits the road. However, the barriers crop up throughout the value process, and preventing them involves a range of functions across the seller's organization. All functions within the organization must recognize their contribution to and their responsibility for the success of your Prime Solution. One of the ways to make this happen is to designate who holds the primary responsibility for resolving or preventing the barriers at any given point in the value creation cycle, and how handoffs

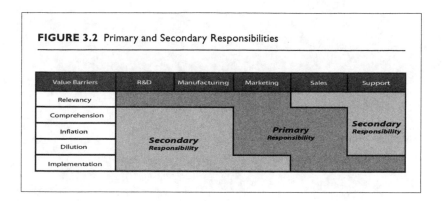

FIGURE 3.2 Primary and Secondary Responsibilities

of responsibility should be conducted as you move through a product development cycle or a value delivery cycle.

Consider the following as a model from which you can designate responsibilities within your organization. The Relevancy Barrier, for example, is located in the value creation phase. The primary responsibility can flow from R&D to manufacturing and on to marketing. The Inflation and Comprehension Barriers are located in the diagnose and design phases and involve marketing and sales. The Dilution and Implementation Barriers are located in the design and delivery phases and should be closely managed by sales and support/service.

This range of functional involvement explains why overcoming the five barriers and closing the Value Gap requires an organizationwide approach. Solution sellers can't simply "fix" the sales organization or bolster the resources devoted to the service/support function and expect solutions failures to disappear. They need an integrated, holistic value process capable of developing and delivering robust, failure-proof solutions. The next three chapters define the characteristics and protocols of such Prime Solutions.

PRIME SOLUTIONS AND THEIR PROTOCOLS

Prime Solutions: integrated offerings of complex products and services that impact the customer's organization at the highest level, enable high-quality buying decisions, and ensure the achievement, sustainability, and measurement of value.

Prime Solutions come in an infinite number of forms and are created for a wide variety of business-to-business markets, but they all encompass three protocols.

1. *Value maximization.* In developing Prime Solutions, we must identify the business drivers that critically concern our customers, address the absence of value, and link our solution to customers' business strategy and goals.
2. *Decision acuity.* In the marketing and selling of Prime Solutions, we need to provide a collaborative decision process that enables customers to diagnose and define the absence of our value, design a solution that will deliver optimal value impact, establish selection criteria, and finally, verify and select the solution that best fits their criteria.
3. *Implementation optimization.* In the delivery of Prime Solutions, we play an integral role in the management of implementation risks, the optimization of the value achieved, and provision of value measurement, sustainability, and enhancement.

4

VALUE LEVERAGE FOR BUSINESS PERFORMANCE

The first protocol of Prime Solutions is value maximization. It is through this mechanism that a Prime Solution leverages your organization's value capabilities or your "sources of value" to positively impact your customer's organization at the highest possible level.

Complex solutions can deliver benefits to customers at three levels of value: product, process, and performance. The source of customer value at the product level derives from the quality, availability, and cost of the product or service itself. At the process level, the source of value is your capability to improve the customer's internal operations. At the highest level of value leverage, the performance level, the solution impacts the customers' corporate business drivers and is tied to their strategic objectives, resulting in the creation of distinct business advantages in their marketplaces.

When a Prime Solution is designed, marketed, and implemented, it leverages value across all three levels of the spectrum. The most significant impact and the highest return, for both you and your customer, reside within the performance level. To create a solution that delivers value at the performance level, you must be able to do the following:

- Understand your customer's business environment and their market drivers (the markets and drivers that critically concern them).
- Identify and address the absence of value (the consequences and costs that your customer experiences in the absence of your solution).
- Link your solution to your customer's existing business strategies and goals, and help them to adjust their strategies and expand their goals as they recognize the solution capabilities you can provide.

These three tasks focus on the customer. We cannot leverage our complex solutions and organizational capabilities unless we can define, address, and connect with value *on our customer's terms*.

The rewards of this level of effort can be considerable. United Parcel Service, Inc., for example, is earning billions in new revenue and has created a promising new business in the service parts logistics (SPL) marketplace.

Efficient and cost-effective SPL is of critical concern to many of UPS's corporate customers, particularly those in high-tech markets. Take semiconductor production equipment, for instance. When this equipment fails in a fabrication plant, the average cost of the downtime is $100,000 per hour. Thus, the speed at which the replacement part is delivered so that the repair can be completed is of paramount importance. In fact, service level agreements often specify response times as short as two hours.

This same level of service urgency is present in a variety of other markets. In fact, global corporate spending aimed at reducing the costs of downtime was an estimated $23 billion in 2003 and is growing at 7 percent annually.[1]

After UPS began developing more sophisticated, value-added shipping solutions aimed at improving the efficiency of its corporate customers' supply chains, it quickly realized that SPL was an issue with which many companies were struggling. The development and maintenance of a global parts network is rarely, if ever, a core competency of the companies that UPS serves, and the costs of an internally developed supply network, which can never reach economies of scale, are high. On further investigation, UPS also found that the market was large enough to offer an attractive return on investment and was currently served by a diverse group of small specialty shippers. In other words, UPS discovered the absence of value and the accompanying high-cost impact, a significant marketplace demand, and to make it all sweeter, a lack of serious competition.

In response, UPS decided to create a solution to the SPL dilemma. Through acquisitions and the leverage of its existing capabilities, the shipping giant quickly created a network of over 550 field stocking facilities on six continents. It also built an IT structure that offered its customers end-to-end visibility as well as leading-edge inventory management tools that ensured that their SPL investment would be as cost-effective as possible.

This Prime Solution quickly attracted customers, such as Silicon Graphics, Compaq, and Tokyo Electron America, who were happy to outsource the service parts support function of SPL. Then UPS took its solution a step further and used the impetus and enthusiasm generated by its initial successes to deepen its service offering, until it was capable of running the entire SPL process, even providing skilled technical personnel.

The result: Between 1996 and 2003, UPS built and grew a $2.5 billion dollar business by leveraging its sources of value and creating Prime Solutions around supply chain challenges representing a compelling absence of value. Currently, this revenue represents approximately 8.5 percent of the global shipper's total annual revenue. It is the company's fastest growing business segment, and unsurprisingly, UPS leadership sees it as the company's most promising growth opportunity.[2]

CLOSE TO THE CUSTOMER

Creating complex solutions that hit the sweet spot in a market requires that we adopt a customercentric approach. This is, of course, so obvious that it has become a truism. Everyone knows that they must be "customer focused," "customercentric," and "close to the customer."

The odd thing about these phrases is that they are so often heard, their meaning has become obscured or, perhaps, purposely subverted. In studying companies that sell complex solutions, we find that, although virtually everyone contends they are working hard to get close to their customers, the purpose behind this work is often misconstrued. More often than not, marketers take a consumer or mass marketing approach. They assume that the customer can and has self-diagnosed their problem, and when a superior solution is presented, the sale will happen.

Their approach becomes clear when you ask sellers about the information they collect from customers. Too often, they are busy attempting to discover information about the customer's past purchases, their plans for future purchases, the size of their purchasing budget, and the process and timeframe in which the customer plans to spend it.

These are standard prospect qualification metrics. When you fill out an application for a free subscription to the typical trade magazine, you are asked these same questions. The magazine tabulates the answers and uses them to sell advertising. As a business-to-business seller, you might very well buy advertising space based on access to tens of thousands of "qualified" subscribers, but would you buy a single name at random, make an appointment, and launch into a presentation?

In reality, when many sellers approach a potential customer, this is exactly the type of information they try to extract. They are "getting close" for the sole purpose of qualifying the customer for a sales pitch. Customers, by the way, figured this out long ago, see it as a waste of their time, and limit access for that very reason. This creates a downward spiral of increasingly negative responses, in which sellers press harder for information and customers shut down communication.

Getting close to the customer is not about qualifying and making a sale. Sellers who persist in this attitude are skipping from the first page of a business book to the last page and then suggesting that they have read the book. The purpose of getting close to customers is to understand what value means *to that customer*. We need to understand what challenges customers are facing, their strategies and priorities in addressing those challenges, and what they are trying to accomplish. We should also understand our customer's market, the challenges *their* customers are facing, and what our customer is trying to help them accomplish. When this type of information is successfully uncovered and used to form the design and delivery of our solutions, the end result is a long-term capability to create value for our customers and capture our fair share of that value for our companies.

The UPS Supply Chain Solution group did not create a service parts logistics solution and then, as an afterthought, go looking for qualified customers. Nor did they ask customers what they were looking to buy. It thoroughly explored the challenges with which its corporate customers were struggling and created a solution that met their SPL needs. It created value on its customers' terms by offering significant improvements in critical response times and the cost reductions inherent in scale. In short, UPS created a source of value that their customers would not likely have thought up on their own and certainly

FIGURE 4.1 The Two Kinds of Information That Sellers Attempt to Get from
Customers

Qualification Metrics	Value Metrics
External Profile	Internal Profile
Usability	Relevancy
Interest	Indicators
Budget	Cost of the Problem Cost of the Solution
Value Proposition	Absence of Value
Approval Process	Decision Process
Product Specification	Performance Metrics

would not have asked for specifically. The objective of the exercise was to understand and create value. The outcome was a capability that could be sold.

The distinction between qualification metrics and value metrics is important, and it can mean the difference between solution success and failure. Take Dean Kamen's much heralded and truly innovative Dynamic Stabilization System. One day, Kamen saw a man struggling to get his wheelchair up a curb and realized its many limitations. He decided to invent a better wheelchair.

Kamen created a new kind of stabilization system, based on self-balancing gyroscopes, which would allow a wheelchair to climb a curb. Johnson & Johnson bought the rights to market Kamen's wheelchair and, with him, spent the next eight years developing the Independence IBOT.

The IBOT, which gained FDA approval and was released in late 2003, is a $29,000 mobility system whose value to the customer is dramatic. Journalist Steve Kemper described its impact like this.

[IBOT] was a super-duper wheelchair that could roll through gravel and sand, go up curbs, and even climb stairs. Most amazingly, it could rise up on its back wheels and roll along in balance. That's what always made the disabled test drivers cry, the simple dignity they reclaimed by "standing up" and looking people in the eye.[3]

The value metrics of the customer were clearly met by IBOT, but Kamen didn't stop there. During the development of the wheelchair, he realized that his unique balancing system could be used to create an entirely new kind of device—a two-wheeled, battery-powered human transporter that the driver can ride standing up. Today, we know it as the Segway.

Everyone working on the Segway loved it. So did a select group of investors, such as venture capitalist John Doerr and Apple Computer's Steve Jobs, who were bowled over by the "coolness" of the Segway and invested over $100 million in the project. It is an amazing device. Lean forward, it moves forward. Lean to the side, it turns. Straighten up, it stops. Doerr was predicting that Segway would "reach $1 billion in sales faster than any start-up in history."[4]

But what were the value metrics of the Segway? Because Kamen insisted on the highest levels of security to protect his new invention, no one ever found out about it. "When I was there," said Steve Kemper in a *Harvard Management Update* interview, "they had almost no marketing research."[5]

This proved to be a significant problem, because Segway's value was never as clear as IBOT's. It didn't enable its owners to do anything they couldn't already do; it only offered an alternative. As an alternative, the Segway also came with some barriers of its own. For example, it was costly, with a retail price starting around $4,000; it required training to use; its battery had a limited operating capacity; and before it could be used on public sidewalks, local governments had to approve it.

The qualification metrics, on the other hand, seduced the Segway team. Everyone has to walk; everyone has to drive short distances. Cities are brimming with people who might decide to use a Segway instead of a cab or the subway. As Kamen and his investors imagined the possibilities, the value promise got larger and larger, until the Segway appeared to be a climactic breakthrough in the history of transportation. But that promise was never tested or confirmed with its prospective customers. In fact, there never was a verified absence of value in the market and, thus, the incentive to change didn't exist.

There certainly were lots of qualified customers for Segway, but as it turned out, there are far fewer actual buyers for the value it offered. Customers have not viewed Segway as a must-have breakthrough solution. Instead, they see it as an innovative and very expensive scooter. The company expected to sell between 50,000 and 100,000 Segways in the first year of production and believed demand would grow from there. As it turned out, approximately 6,000 units were sold.[6]

VALUE DRIVERS AS PERFORMANCE METRICS

In the business-to-business world, the most evident and most relevant performance metrics can be found in the customer's value drivers. Value drivers represent the goals customers have set and the internal and external challenges that they face. The drivers offer sellers insights necessary to get beyond qualification and, instead, craft solutions that connect to the highest level of customer value.

Customer value drivers are not difficult to uncover. Most companies have adopted a "what you measure is what you get" approach, so they tend to track the drivers or performance metrics that reflect their critical business objectives. These objectives show up in corporate scorecards, annual reports, and Web sites.

In the effort to get their entire company focused and energized around specific goals, CEOs constantly talk about value drivers and often refer to them in media interviews and other public statements. If the CEO has succeeded in conveying this message, any manager within the CEO's organization should be able to reel off their short-term and long-term business priorities.

The value drivers of your customers' customers also yield insight into performance metrics. Your customers are, or should be, vitally concerned with helping their customers achieve value. When you create a solution that enables a customer to add value to *their* solutions, engaging their undivided attention becomes much easier.

Today's customers utilize many different performance metric systems: witness the widespread adoption of balanced scorecards, key performance indicators, critical success factors, and the classic—management by objectives. One of the most serious contributors to the Value Gap is the imprecise connection between customer performance metrics and solution capabilities.

To make this connection more manageable, we found that the majority of business objectives or business drivers will fall into three categories—financial, quality, and competitive. Understanding how your solutions and the value you can deliver impacts each of these three categories will provide an efficient and precise method to connect your value to your customer's performance metrics.

Financial drivers. There are two financial drivers: revenues and expenses.

Revenues focus on top-line growth. Solutions that increase income through the creation of new businesses, marketplace expansion, expanded product/service offerings, and innovative new products would impact a revenue-driven customer.

Expenses focus on bottom-line growth via decreased costs. Solutions that reduce inventory, improve efficiency, speed processes, lower cost of goods sold, and/or lower overhead would impact the expense driver of a customer.

Quality drivers. There are three quality drivers: customer satisfaction, employee satisfaction, and regulatory compliance.

Customer satisfaction is a common driver aimed at capturing the proven benefits of fulfilling customer needs and desires. Solutions that reduce product defects, improve product performance, streamline the customer experience, or retain and expand customer relationships would impact customer satisfaction.

Employee satisfaction is a driver aimed at supporting the human side of the corporate equation. Solutions that increase employee productivity, make operations easier, increase retention levels, or improve recruiting results would impact employee satisfaction.

Regulatory compliance is aimed at meeting the external requirements of a business. Solutions that enable compliance with legislation, such as the Sarbanes-Oxley Act of 2002, or speed FDA approval of new medications would impact a regulatory compliance-driven customer.

Competitive drivers. The two competitive drivers are uniqueness and availability. These value drivers create an impact for customers in *their* marketplaces.

Uniqueness is about creating products and services that offer a competitive advantage and a distinct differentiator in the customer's marketplace. Solutions that enable the development of a new product format or an expanded service that no other competitor has would impact a customer who is driving to establish a unique position.

The availability driver focuses on how offerings are delivered to the marketplace. Solutions that enable new avenues of distribution or more efficient manufacturing or delivery would impact a customer driving toward higher levels of availability.

FIGURE 4.2 Value Driver Chart

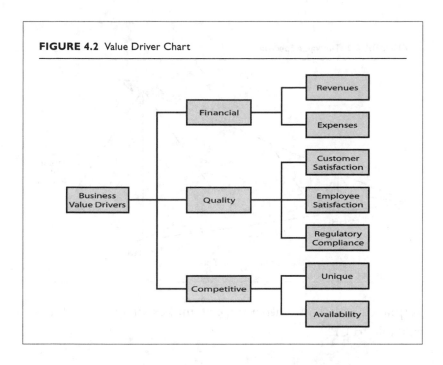

The value impact of a Prime Solution is raised as it connects to multiple drivers. The Prophet by Baxter parts-planning software, developed by Baxter Planning Systems in Austin, Texas, provides a good example. This sophisticated software estimates inventory levels, parts demand based on product lifecycles and other considerations, and geographic need. In 2002, UPS's Service Parts Logistics unit announced that it would use Baxter's software to expand its services.[7]

Why did Baxter win this business? Looking through the filter of value drivers, we would suggest that their solution connected to multiple performance metrics at UPS. The software creates a unique competitive advantage and increased revenue by attracting new business to the shipper's SPL unit. It impacted expenses by rightsizing the shipper's global parts storage network. It improved customer satisfaction by rightsizing UPS's customers' inventory investments and improving service levels to their customers. And it impacted the uniqueness driver by enhancing and differentiating UPS's service offering in the mar-

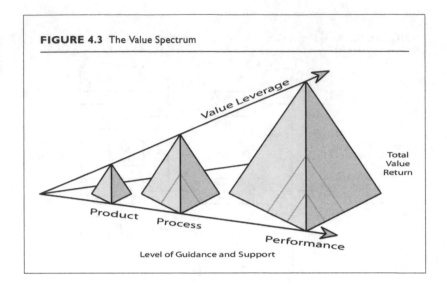

FIGURE 4.3 The Value Spectrum

ketplace. This cumulative impact makes Prophet by Baxter valuable to UPS.

THE VALUE SPECTRUM

The clearer and more frequent the connections between a solution and customer value drivers, the higher the solution moves on the Value Spectrum and the more value leverage it creates. As introduced in the opening of this chapter, the Value Spectrum has three levels—product, process, and performance. It is important to understand the three levels and design your solutions to encompass all three whenever possible to impact as high a level as possible.

1. *Product.* The source of customer value at the product level is inherent in the characteristics of the product itself. These include its quality, availability, and cost. Solutions whose value is restricted to the product level are usually seen and treated as commodities in the marketplace. Acquisition cost often becomes the primary factor

in the purchase decision. The seller is usually viewed as one vendor among many and generally does not have a great deal of customer interaction beyond contact with the purchasing function.

2. *Process.* At the process level, the source of value moves outside the solution itself and focuses on the impact of the product or service on the customer's business processes. The solution now has a value to the customer that extends beyond its base characteristics into the efficacy of the processes within the customer's organization. The purchase decision is elevated to a consideration of cost of goods sold, production efficiency, and customer satisfaction, all of which are value drivers that can be impacted by helping customers improve their processes. Customers now see you as a limited partner who works with various operational executives, department heads, and the organizations that they lead.

3. *Performance.* At the performance level, the solution delivers an impact to the performance and differentiation of the customer's product, beyond the customer's internal processes and into its marketplaces and its customers' worlds. The solution takes on a strategic value to the customer. Here, the solution creates value that enables your customer to serve their customers better, provides distinct competitive differentiation, adds to the significance and definition of their brand, and, perhaps, expands their markets. The customer's decision is now elevated to the consideration of revenue enhancement and strategy fulfillment. In the customer's mind, you now become a strategic business partner and, as such, interact with their senior and executive leadership.

The performance level, located at the highest end of the Value Spectrum, represents the highest level of customer value achievement and has the potential to be transformational to your customer's business. Prime Solutions leverage your value promise and your customer's value achievement to bring about the performance level.

Atlanta-based Georgia-Pacific Resins, Inc. (GPRI), a subsidiary of paper and building products giant Georgia-Pacific Corporation, provides an excellent example of how to apply leverage to evolve solutions along the Value Spectrum.[8] GPRI is squarely positioned in what many businesspeople would define as a commodity market. It makes a number of industrial chemical products, including thermosetting resins used as manufacturing adhesives, chemicals to impact paper performance, and formaldehyde—all sold by weight or volume.

The baseline for GPRI's industry is value at the product level. At that level of value, the company works to provide high-quality resins—resins that are consistent in their composition, free of contamination, delivered on time, invoiced accurately, etc. The value of the resin is relegated to these characteristics and the acquisition cost. GPRI's customers understand the resin's value but often do not view it as substantially different from competing resins. Customers focus on lowering the price of the resin, clearly limiting the source of value to reducing their raw material cost. Thus, purchasing is the transaction manager, and pricing becomes highly competitive.

But GPRI has developed solutions that have an impact beyond the products themselves. For example, the company is operating at the process level when it analyzes its customers' manufacturing processes and then creates adhesives that enable customers to manufacture their products more efficiently, thereby increasing output of the customer facility while lowering per unit fixed costs. This delivers far more value to the customer and substitutes the price arguments of the product level with alternative savings resulting from the process improvement. GPRI has expanded the customer relationship from the single point of contact with the purchasing department and is working with the customer's operations and sales management that are impacted by the efficiency of the manufacturing process.

GPRI leverages value further when it develops products that enable its customers to develop new and improved products. The company is operating in the performance range when it creates a chemical coating that alters the characteristics of its customer's product. By creating a coating that expands the utility of its customer's products, GPRI has enabled its customer to open new markets and/or expand their margins in existing markets. Now, the company is working with the customer at the enterprise level as a strategic partner. It has made a significant positive impact on its customer's overall business performance, an impact that is measurably beyond what could be done by offering the customer a lower price on the coating.

Prime Solution sellers are maximizing the impact range of their products and services through each step in the process of delivering solutions to customers. As we will see in greater detail in Part Three, R&D uses the Value Spectrum in the solution development process. It is also used by marketing to successfully segment and introduce the solution to its markets. It is used by sales to structure its approach to individual customers, and it is used by service/support to implement the solution, measure its results, and drive the enhancement of value achievement.

When you begin firing on all cylinders in this way, you move far beyond those competitors who are thinking only at the product level, abandoning their customers at the point of delivery.

THREE FINAL QUESTIONS

To summarize, successful business-to-business sellers maximize value by living in their customers' worlds and creating solutions from that perspective. They connect the value of their solutions to multiple business drivers within their customers' organizations, then leverage the value those solutions provide across the Value Spectrum to the performance level.

All of this work can be verified and validated with three questions that must be answered together. They provide a simple sanity check that ensures that the fundamental elements of value maximization have been fully considered.

1. *From your perspective, what are your sources of differentiated value?* The sources of solution value reside within your organization and encompass the impact of your products and services. They are the development partnerships that you create to differentiate and extend your value creation capabilities. The answers to this first question confirm that your organization has considered and clarified all of its capabilities and competencies that can add unique value to a customer's business.

2. *From your customer's perspective, what are your customer's uses of your value?* The fact that your organization can deliver value is no assurance that the solution will resonate with the value drivers of your customers. So answering the second question will ensure that the sources of value within your organization are aligned with your customer's uses of value, as specified by their value drivers. When you understand the customer's uses of value, you can create solutions that touch all levels of the Value Spectrum.

3. *What are the indicators of and costs of the absence of value?* Once the uses of value are identified, its absence and the consequences thereof must be quantified. You will not be able to identify the best customers for a solution until you know what the customer's world looks like when the solution is not in place. In other words, how and where specifically does the absence of your value physically manifest within a customer's organization? What has

your customer experienced in the past, what might they be experiencing right now, or what might they experience in the future in the absence of your value?

This is what we call *indicators of the absence of value.* These indicators are physical signs. They are the evidence of the absence of value and can be detected and, most importantly, measured. You cannot properly value a solution until you know the financial impact of its absence.

Answering these three questions will ensure the validity of your solution value. They confirm that all of your organization's value capabilities have been tied to relevant value drivers within your target market. Therefore, you can be assured that there is a valid market for your solution and that it is possible to identify and quantify the absence of the value you provide to an individual customer. When all of those conditions are met, the first protocol of a Prime Solution has been completed.

5

MULTIPLE DECISIONS, MUTUAL UNDERSTANDINGS

The second protocol of a Prime Solution is decision acuity. Decision acuity begins by recognizing the multiple dimensions of a high-quality decision. A high-quality decision is more than just a decision to buy; it is a decision about priorities, change, investment, commitment, and risk. It creates a secure foundation for predictable value achievement.

This protocol empowers customers with a clear understanding of their problems, including the overall impact and cost of those problems. Further, it provides a method for understanding the opportunities available, arms them with the knowledge and insight necessary to evaluate solution alternatives, and equips them to achieve realistic results. By providing a decision process and guidance, it also positions you and your organization as a trusted and valued decision partner in the customer's eyes.

As we've already seen, customers' decision-making competencies vary widely in the complex business arena. While there are a small number of highly knowledgeable customers in any given market, business executives and managers typically are not well equipped to make high-quality decisions regarding every facet of their business and the multitude of solution alternatives. This situation creates a valuable opportunity for solution providers.

Sellers tend to approach this opportunity from one of three ascending relationship levels: reactive, proactive, or interactive. At the reactive level, sellers comply with the customer's buying process with little or no question. They do not question the customer's situation or objectives. They merely comply with the customer's request for information (i.e., the RFP).

At the proactive level, sellers arrive with a preplanned, fixed process. This process is characterized by superficial questioning so that the salesperson is informed enough to suggest a solution. It relies on the customer's ability to self-diagnose, and its goal is to align problem to solution.

At the highest level of the relationship—the interactive level—solution providers focus on expanding the customer's understanding of their own problem and alternatives. These sellers bring a process that encompasses guidance for and collaboration with the customer in pursuit of a high-quality decision.

As with the maximization of solution value, we can think of these as levels in a Decision Spectrum. When a Prime Solution is developed, an interactive decision process is also designed and aligned with it. To create a decision process capable of operating at the interactive relationship level, sellers must be able to do the following:

- Overcome the obstacles imposed by conventional selling and buying processes and unite their entire organization around the best interests of the customer.
- Recognize that a decision to buy is a decision to change.

- Create an incentive to change through the analysis and quantification of the cost of the problem, the cost of the solution, and the net value created.
- Establish the confidence to invest by reducing the customer's risk of change and increasing the probability of a successful solution.

Again, we should note that the customer is the natural locus of these tasks. The customer makes the ultimate decision. As with medicine, the doctor may make a strong recommendation, but the patient still has the final say. Solution providers are best equipped to construct, manage, and influence the decision process, but that process will not work unless it is aligned with the customer's interests and undertaken with the customer's consent. A process that does not fulfill those requirements is neither authentic nor legitimate.

THE REACTIVE SELLER

The first level of the Decision Spectrum is populated by reactive sellers. At this level, the customer's process becomes the basis for the buying decision. Customers bring their own process to the transaction when considering complex solutions, because historically they have not been able to rely on sellers to represent their interests.

These defense-oriented buying processes generally have as many flaws as the conventional selling process. By definition, complex solutions do *not* lend themselves to analysis and comparison via a standardized buying process. Therefore, to have a reasonable chance of successfully identifying the best complex solution, buyers would need a process designed for and dedicated to that solution category. This task might well cost buyers more in resources, time, and energy than they would save in the effort.

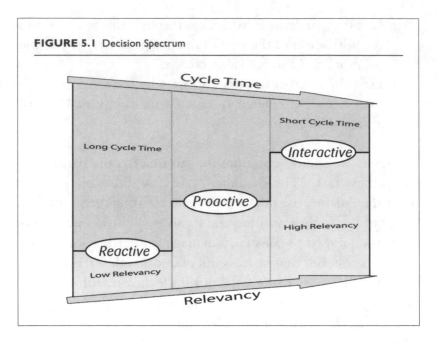

FIGURE 5.1 Decision Spectrum

As a result, most buying processes try to force complex, highly differentiated solution alternatives into a simplistic, apples-to-apples comparison. This artificial comparison typically serves neither the buyer nor the seller. Instead, it usually leads directly to a collision with the Dilution Barrier (see Chapter 2), because the selling price becomes the only significant common denominator that the buyer can pinpoint, and sellers respond by stripping value out of the solution to meet price constraints.

To be fair, many solution buyers recognize that value is more important than price. Further, in recent years, advanced purchasing techniques and strategies have been developed to undertake the comparison of complex solutions. But the reality of the complex solutions arena is that the best source of knowledge to understand these solutions and the situations in which they are applicable, especially in emerging markets such as RFID, resides with the solution providers. In the end, a buyer-led process has poor prospects of producing a high-quality decision and establishing a solid foundation for value achievement.

THE PROACTIVE SELLER

The proactive level of the Decision Spectrum is populated by sellers who vainly attempt to apply (what should be) an obsolete "prospect, qualify, present, and close" approach to complex solutions (with a heavy emphasis on "present and close"). The odds of success with this agenda are stacked against proactive sellers; they are struggling to use an Era One process to connect with Era Three customers.

Herbert W. Lovelace, the pseudonym of a CIO who is a regular contributor to *InformationWeek,* humorously described the problems inherent in the conventional sales process in a column aptly titled "Trapped in the Sales Presentation from Hell."[1] The presentation in question was one that was delivered to Lovelace by a sales manager in his own company. The manager was preparing to meet a potential customer with whom the CIO was acquainted and asked Lovelace to critique his presentation.

Lovelace tries to enlighten the sales manager about the prospect's notable lack of patience and asks how much time has been allotted for the presentation. "As long as it takes," blusters the sales manager. "We have a good story to tell!" Lovelace goes on to describe the hour-long presentation as "painful." He listened to a 15-minute recitation of his company's history followed by "mind-numbing detail about our manufacturing processes."

The sales manager proceeds and meets with the prospect anyway, and unsurprisingly, no new business materializes. The sales manager's response to this outcome is to say that the prospect "doesn't have the vision to understand the value of strategic relationships."

Lovelace's account is a dramatic illustration of the problem with proactive sales processes. They simply do not develop enough depth of information about the customer's world to ensure a quality decision. They are about the seller, the solution, and the promise of value. They require that buyers understand their own complex problems (sometimes problems that they didn't even know they had) and, with little or no assistance, comprehend all of the ramifications of the offered solutions.

Worse, when they are designed for the sole benefit of the seller, the proactive sales processes become adversarial. Customers become pawns to be manipulated. If customers do not respond to the salesperson's liking, they get coerced (a more accurate description of what actually happens when a customer hesitates or pushes back than "overcoming objections"). The customer's interests are usually poorly represented. At its worst, the goal of the proactive sales process is a signed deal, not the customer's value achievement. Not to oversimplify, but the reactive level is about the customer's buying process and the proactive level is about the seller's sales process. The only substantive difference between these two levels of the Decision Spectrum is who is in control.

THE INTERACTIVE DECISION TEAM

The answer to the shortcomings of reactive and proactive processes is to recast them into a single, decision-based process that serves both you and your customer with a mutually agreed objective. In a Prime Solution scenario, you and your customers can use this process to travel through the multiple decisions that must be navigated in a complex sale; create mutual understanding and goals around your customer's situation and the best solution to address it; and ensure a secure foundation for value achievement, both now and in the future. This kind of process operates in the interactive range of the Decision Spectrum and creates decision acuity.

The Graham Company, the commercial insurance brokerage that we introduced in the first chapter, provides an excellent example of how providing decision acuity can become a competitive advantage in the marketplace.[2] The insurance

products that Graham represents are not substantially different from the products offered by other commercial insurance
brokerages, nor do product costs vary significantly between
brokerages.

There is, however, infinite variation in both the coverage
requirements and cost parameters of the customers *and* the
way in which insurance contracts are written and combined to
create a comprehensive solution. In terms of these variables,
the process that supports the customer's decision is where the
rubber meets the road for a commercial brokerage. That decision process is also what differentiates Graham from its competitors.

The brokerage invests a great deal of time and resources in
ensuring that the customer makes the best decision possible.
Vice president of sales Kevin McPoyle explains:

> Our process is designed to provide meaningful
> guidance by getting precise information directly from
> the plant floor. We work on very complex industries
> such as construction, chemical manufacturing, and spe-
> cialty manufacturing. We don't simply assume what the
> prospect's perspective is on risk and exposure. We will
> visit facilities anywhere in the world to understand
> their business firsthand. We bring in our highly trained
> staff to find out everything we can about the business
> and the exposures that exist in the business. We want to
> talk to everyone who may have input, from defining the
> risk, to setting the risk management strategy, to the se-
> lection of an insurance broker—that means everyone
> from the department managers to the financial staff to
> the CEO. We want to know what they are experiencing
> and what their concerns are so we can address them. If
> they stay in our process, we are able to continue show-
> ing where they have problems and how we can help
> solve those problems.

This level of decision interaction does not normally come cheap. If the industry's leading consulting organization were contracted to do it, it could cost the prospect as much $75,000. McPoyle continues:

> We do not charge for the process, because it establishes our credibility and provides the opportunity to look deep inside an organization. More often than not, the potential client's leaders are amazed and aghast at what we know and what they don't about their own business risks. During the diagnosis, we often find 80 to 90 coverage problems with a prospect's existing program. During the design phase, we can usually correct about 90 percent of these coverage issues with the current insurance carrier.

In the end, however, Graham's results justify its investment in this interactive decision process. They do not classify it as "unpaid consulting." The customer "pays" for this guidance on the front end by providing access to all the required people and information. A clear view of coverage exposures and the best solution alternatives enables Graham's clients to make high-quality risk management decisions. Nearly 80 percent of the time, the prospect becomes a Graham client. Compare that to the industry's average conversion rate of 15 percent.

Graham offers an interactive decision process that serves both seller and buyer. The adversarial confrontations that result as unavoidable by-products of conventional processes are eliminated, as sellers and buyers are united in a single process.

Just as important, the desired outcomes of conventional processes are not lost. For the seller, the goal of the conventional selling process—to provide complex solutions that deliver value—still exists in an interactive process. For buyers, the goal of conventional buying processes—to find the most cost-effective solution to the problem—still exists. The focus, however, has changed from the transaction itself—the purchase or sale—to the quality of the decision and the probability of a successful outcome.

A FORMULA FOR A
HIGH-QUALITY DECISION

It is a foregone conclusion that the decision to purchase and implement a whole solution will be a complicated undertaking. The sophistication and ramifications of complex solutions and the extent and implications of complex problems combine virtually to guarantee that complex decisions have to be made. Unfortunately, the teams that customers assemble internally to consider, influence, and decide complex solution purchases are often not particularly adept at complex decision making

In addition to an understandable lack of expertise in the problems and solutions they are considering, customer's teams are subject to all the flaws and foibles of group-based decision making. There are many obstacles to sound decisions, including fear of change and risk, the pressure to conform, and the hypnotic effect of majority opinions.

Crossfunctional dysfunction represents one of the most flagrant and disruptive obstacles to sound decisions. One of the most common manifestations of this problem occurs when functions have conflicting incentives—for instance, when a purchasing department may have an incentive to reduce acquisition costs, with no accountability for value dilution at the operations level.

Even the desire to make the best decision can be an obstacle to sound decision making, according to Princeton University's Daniel Kahneman, one of the leading experts on the subject. The Nobel Prize–winning professor explains that decision analysis is predicated on the fact that there is no "right" decision; all solution alternatives are, to one degree or another, a gamble. He says:

> Managers think of themselves as captains of a ship on a stormy sea. Risk for them is danger, but they are fighting it—very controlled. The idea that you are gambling is an admission that, at a certain point, you have lost control and you have no control beyond a certain point. That is abhorrent to decision managers; that's why they reject decision analysis.[3]

Kahneman, along with Dan Lovallo of the Australian Graduate School of Management at the University of New South Wales, also found that poor business decisions are often caused by "delusional optimism." There is, they explained, a natural human tendency to exaggerate our own chances of success. In business decisions, the tendency to think in terms of best-case scenarios is reinforced by organizational and cultural pressures, such as stretch goals, loyalty, and the need to paint a rosy picture to secure funding. The results: "delusions of success" and, ultimately, unexpected problems, time and cost overruns, and project failures. [4]

An interactive decision process is designed to anticipate and avoid problems such as these. Its aim is always the reduction of risk, but it does not promise the elimination of risk. It cannot, because there are no free moves in complex sales. There is some degree of risk in every solution alternative, and you will always give up something when you reject an alternative. The solution provider's job is to ensure that the customer's decision embodies that fact and is based on a realistic recognition of those risks.

An interactive decision process also provides a powerful antidote to the decision-making viruses that thrive in what Kahneman and Lovallo call the "inside view." Instead of preying on the natural optimism of buyers, a solution provider with an interactive process provides a constructive view from outside the customer's decision team. That view encompasses not only the dedicated expertise of the solution provider, and all the relevant information and perspectives residing inside the customer's organization, but also provides all the data that the solution provider has gathered from the experiences of previous customers. This "outside view" provides a reference group for assessment that Kahneman and Lovallo say is indispensable to sound decision making.

The formula for an interactive decision is the right people asking the right questions in the right sequence. The right people—drawn from both the customer's and the resource provider's organizations—ensure that the outside view is properly considered. The right questions in the right sequence give structure to the decision process and ensure that the smoke and mirrors caused by competition and internal politics do not obscure the process.

PERSPECTIVE AND THE INTERACTIVE DECISION

The success of the right people portion of the interactive decision formula hinges on the critical characteristic of perspective. Solution providers need to consider the issue of perspective in two contexts. First, they must ensure that the decision team is populated with all of the various perspectives required to thoroughly diagnose and quantify the customer's problem, as well as the perspectives required to understand the customer's solution alternatives. Second, to be fully comprehensible, the information that is developed must speak clearly to the various perspectives of the decision makers.

Let's start with the first requirement: just like any successful play or movie, a successful decision requires a cast of characters that can do justice to its subject. This cast is drawn from both the buyer's and seller's organizations.

Today's complex solution providers need to recognize that even their own salespeople often do not have all of the expertise required to understand a customer's problems and all of the intricacies of the offered solution. Providers should ensure that their side of the decision team includes a complete cast. The Graham Company, for instance, routinely sends risk managers, attorneys, CPAs, and industry experts into sales engagements. These cast members ensure that exposures and risks, which are often hidden within a customer's company, are identified and addressed.

Complex solution providers must also consider the customer's side of the decision team. Too often, salespeople and their companies overlook this task, leaving it to customers to identify and assign their own cast members. This is a mistake—if customers do not yet have the expertise required to understand the parameters of a complex problem and its solution alternatives, they are also not yet capable of choosing an effective decision cast.

Companies who provide Prime Solutions step into this breach and assist the customer in selecting their cast of characters. They identify and recruit cast members from the customer's organization who have the information, impact, influence, and insight needed to undertake an interactive decision process. Graham takes the selection of the customer's cast very seriously. In fact, the broker will withdraw from a sales engagement if a customer denies access to employees who are critical to a complete diagnosis as well as a fully informed decision.

Now to the second requirement of perspective: just as important as recruiting the proper cast of characters is the task of ensuring that the data and recommendations that this team develops will be clearly understood by all those responsible. That includes members of your team as well as the customer's team.

A Prime Solution is actively connected to the perspective of each listener. It is described in terms that directly and clearly speak to the concerns of individuals. In business, perspective is usually intimately related to the individual's job responsibilities. For example, in discussing the impact of a manufacturing inefficiency on a customer's financial performance, the conversation with the CEO would likely focus on earnings per share and gross revenue. The same information would be translated into quarterly production cost for a divisional executive and into cost per unit for an operational manager.

Matching the message to the listener's perspective is a basic precept of effective marketing. But we are always surprised at how often sellers make the mistake of discussing problems and solutions in terms that do not resonate with their listeners. When sellers leave it up to the listeners to interpret that information on their own, the listeners often either do not bother to make the translation at all or mistranslate the information. When that happens, the integrity of the decision is compromised.

One of our clients, a Germany-based pharmaceutical company, received a firsthand lesson in the power of perspective when it released a new angiotensin converting enzyme (ACE) inhibitor, a drug used to treat high blood pressure and other cardiovascular problems. The new drug was brought to market at a 25 percent discount to competing products, but it was not on insurers' medication formularies. Thus, doctors who prescribed it to insured patients had to apply for exceptions, requiring additional paperwork and time.

The company's sales organization attempted to sell the medication in their usual way. They offered free samples on their calls, and when the doctor signed for the samples, they quickly presented the benefit of the "drug's lower cost." But far fewer doctors than expected prescribed the ACE inhibitor. As we began our consulting, we considered the doctor's perspective on the problem and the real absence of value.

One of the major concerns of any physician is the patient's not following their care plan. In the case of prescription drugs, patients who cannot afford a drug may attempt to stretch their medicine by taking it less often than prescribed. This, of course, negatively impacts the course of treatment and the patient's health. Doctors become concerned with the cost of a drug when it threatens the health of their patient.

So the company's salespeople began asking doctors if they noticed any patients stretching their prescriptions, and if so, whether they were individuals without prescription coverage. When a physician acknowledged that a number of patients fit that description, the salesperson suggested that the new ACE inhibitor might be an effective solution, as there are no formulary restrictions for uninsured patients and the lower cost offers the patient greater buying power. Doctors now had specific patients in mind and agreed to prescribe, and the market share of the new medicine quickly doubled.

This example shows an interactive decision-making process in which a source of value was leveraged to the performance level. The salesperson went beyond product value (lower cost of drug) and process value (actually negative with the additional paperwork cost) to the performance level—in this case, the performance of the doctor's practice through patients' success.

THE INCENTIVE TO CHANGE AND THE CONFIDENCE TO INVEST

Complex solutions typically require major change efforts. For the customer, the decision to undertake changes of this magnitude is neither simple nor familiar. Further, the risk inherent in a solution decision can reach dramatic, bet-the-company proportions. An interactive decision process serves as a change catalyst and a risk manager. This process enables your customer to reduce the risk of connecting their unique situations and problems to the most effective solution alternative. To create this bridge, a decision process must answer two questions.

1. *The incentive to change.* Should the customer act on the problem?
2. *The confidence to invest.* If so, which solution option will bring the most success, in terms of value creation, and the least amount of risk?

In the business-to-business world, these questions must be answered in financial terms. The language of business is money; companies are in business to make money. If no cost is associated with a problem, then there is no problem. Cost can be expressed in a combination of figures: directly with established figures, indirectly with inferred figures, or in terms of lost opportunity (the lost potential of the path not followed). If the customer does not clearly recognize a negative cost impact, they have no incentive to change.

Likewise, the idea of a solution without a cost is ludicrous. Obviously, sellers will reluctantly discuss acquisition costs, but we often see sellers struggling to avoid discussing total solution costs. Instead, they focus on ROI and other future benefits. It is possible to sell a rosy future, but such an approach offers no urgent incentive to change, and any seller who attempts it can expect poor conversion ratios and very long sales cycles. Further, economist Milton Friedman was right when he said, "There's no such thing as a free lunch." Every customer knows that any seller who actually offered a no-cost solution would quickly go out of business.

The salient point is that solution providers need to translate the two decision considerations into quantitative terms. Thus, an interactive decision process seeks to answer two questions: "What is the cost of the problem?" and "What is the cost of the solution?" When the answers are properly calculated and compared, the best decision alternatives become clear.

Cost of the Problem

This part of the decision equation is the one most often missing in the complex solutions world. Sellers are so busy pitching the features, benefits, and ROIs of their solutions, they forget to determine how much discomfort the customer is experiencing in the absence of the solution's value. It is virtually impossible to make a sound decision unless that pain is thoroughly explored, quantified, and realized by the buyer. Buyers need to know the cost of staying the same—the cost of *not* changing.

Determining the cost of the problem essentially requires a process of diagnosis. Like a doctor examining a patient who is not feeling well, the decision team is examining the buyer's situation. This work consists of three elements.

1. *Scoping.* Aimed at uncovering the information and data needed to understand the problem
2. *Analyzing.* Aimed at the extrapolation of research into a calculation of the costs of the problem
3. *Reporting.* Aimed at the interpretation and communication of those findings

When a team scopes a problem, it looks for the common indicators of the problems the solution has been designed to eliminate. This might be manufacturing defects, adverse reactions to a medication, or abandoned shopping carts on a Web site. Once an indicator is found, the entire range of its consequences is identified. The team looks across the organization and asks questions, such as, "Who gets the call when this indicator occurs?," "Who fixes it?," and "Whose performance measurements are impacted?"

Next, the team analyzes the consequences they have identified. It contacts the people who are affected by each of the consequences and tracks the business impact. The costs associated with each consequence are estimated, and a financial impact is attached to each.

Finally, the team reports the findings. The information gathered is summarized, and a figure that represents the total cost of the problem is calculated. The report is discussed with the proper decision team members in terms that are aligned with their individual perspectives. If the cost is significant enough to warrant attention and the priorities of the customer's organization allow for action, we have created the incentive to change, and the team moves forward to the second half of the decision equation.

Cost of the Solution

The cost of the solution process is essentially a process of connection. The team is connecting the diagnosis of the problem to the design of the solution. It is quantifying the cost of change. While sellers are usually happy to discuss the price of a solution, they tend to be much less forthcoming when the issue of true cost arises.

Price is only the first element in the true cost of a complex solution. It is the tag on the box—the cost of getting the solution to the dock.

The second element is the cost of implementation. For instance, we work with a manufacturer of radiation therapy equipment whose solution is priced at around $20 million. The equipment, however, usually requires the construction of a dedicated facility that can cost up to $50 million. Switching costs (a cost that some solution sellers rely on to hold their customers hostage), employee training costs, and process reengineering costs are also significant implementation factors.

The final element is the cost of using the solution. The energy that a solution consumes, the staffing levels it requires, maintenance costs, and user licensing fees are all examples of usage costs and must be included in the total cost of ownership.

In the world of complex solutions, the costs of implementation and use often exceed the selling price. That is why it is impossible to make a sound decision without knowing the total cost of a solution. Once the implementation plan is understood and the total cost of the solution alternatives is established, the customer is enabled to invest with confidence.

This is not an insignificant accomplishment. When you give customers the confidence to invest, they will jump substantial hurdles to invest in your solutions. Witness Shell Global Solutions International BV, The Hague, Netherlands-based subsidiary of the Royal Dutch/Shell Group. Until 1998, Shell Global Solutions was an internal support group that provided research and technical services to the oil giant's operating companies. Today, it is a billion dollar technology business consultancy that works with internal and external customers in a wide variety of industries worldwide.

Shell Global Solutions provides services to most of the world's oil producers and refiners, including many government-owned companies in Central and South America, Asia, and the Middle East. These are companies that are extremely difficult to "sell" in the traditional sense. Mike Mitchell, Shell Global Solutions principal account executive and business node manager, Middle East, says: "Fundamentally, I start from the premise that there will be institutionalized barriers to any complex sale in the majority of customers I will be working with."

It is no wonder. These companies and countries have often been victims of "old school" sales and technology dumping. To protect themselves from unscrupulous salespeople, they have responded with legislation that prohibits single sourcing and inhibits corruption. Unfortunately, this same legislation also makes it difficult to do business with legitimate companies.

Mitchell has found the answer to that problem in what he calls "the compelling story." There is an important distinction here: *a* compelling story will get your company into the customer's office—it is an assumption about value, but no more than that; *the* compelling story is one that is tailored to the customer's business, which provides all the information that the customer requires to make a sound decision.

The compelling story gives a customer the confidence to invest. Shell Global Solutions has seen the power of this confidence firsthand. It has worked with several government-owned companies in the Caribbean and South America that have gone as far as amending public legislation in order to hire the company as a single source provider.[5]

To summarize, a Prime Solution enables decision acuity. It is accompanied by an interactive decision process that brings together solution providers and their customers. Interactive decision processes require trust and transparency between solution providers and buyers. This process develops a full and accurate portrait of the problem *and* solution costs. It enhances the quality of the customer's decision process and gives your customer the "confidence to invest" in your solution. A better decision also reduces the risk of change that comes with every implementation effort—the subject of the final protocol of Prime Solutions.

6

EFFECTIVE EXECUTION, MEASURABLE RESULTS

The third protocol of a Prime Solution is return optimization. Its goal is to ensure that customers maximize the value inherent to the complex solution. The value promise is fulfilled and solution value is made tangible, is measured, and is enhanced through the return optimization mechanism.

In the business-to-business marketplace, return optimization represents the customer's ultimate goal and the bottom-line measure of value. It is also the greatest challenge facing complex solution sellers. Without doubt, buyers are struggling to extract the value from their complex solution purchases. For customers, that struggle takes place *after* the purchase, *after* the implementation, and *after* the seller has moved on to its next prospect. This has created a vacuum, which is manifesting itself in the growing market demand for postpurchase services.

Savvy solution providers are moving aggressively to fill that demand. We've already described how IBM is morphing into a new kind of company, which integrates the traditional product and service business models. Instead of focusing on the products or services themselves, IBM's leaders are focusing on the customer's value achievement and on providing the products and services to support that goal.

Other sellers are undertaking similar transformations. Unisys Corporation has successfully turned its established, products-based business model on its head in the past five years. In 2003, it derived 80 percent of its revenue from service and is pursuing what CEO Larry Weinbach calls "business-process outsourcing," a strategy in which Unisys products and services are combined to deliver value through the management and improvement of an entire process.

Take the ubiquitous bank check, for instance. For the first time, recent legislation allowed U.S. banks to exchange images of checks instead of the physical checks themselves. This enabled a significant reengineering of traditional check processing, and Unisys, whose systems already processed half of all the checks written worldwide, began helping its customers create processes to capture the new value inherent in the change. One result: In late 2002, the company announced a $500 million, seven-year outsourcing contract with financial services company Washington Mutual. The contract called for Unisys to reengineer and manage Washington Mutual's entire check processing operation, including the installation of image-capturing devices in each branch and the operation of regional check processing centers.[1]

Information storage giant EMC Corporation has also focused its attention on what is often considered the customer's end of the value chain. The hardware company's CEO, Joe Tucci, spent $3.5 billion on acquisitions in 2002 and 2003 to add software and services to EMC's solution offerings. From 2004 onward, Tucci wants to give customers the ability to "virtualize" their information storage—that is, to allocate and reallocate EMC's storage systems as the customer's information storage needs change.[2] In essence, EMC is focused on the task of enabling its solutions to deliver value in yet unknown future states.

These companies would not be rushing to assist customers unless the third protocol, return optimization, also offered what may well be the most lucrative opportunity currently available for competitive advantage and a clear path to their own revenue and profit growth. Consider the fast-developing RFID solutions marketplace as an example. A Yankee Group report estimates that the RFID market will grow to $4.2 billion by 2008.[3]

Half of that figure, roughly $2 billion, will be spent on RFID electronic product code tags. The market for these tags will surely be a commodity market—sales are already highly price-sensitive. Tag makers will be forced to squeeze every penny out of their costs and, eventually, their margins.

The other half of the RFID market will be infrastructure. Yankee Group Technology Management Strategies program manager Andy Efstathiou adds, "The largest portion of infrastructure spending will be allocated to consulting and systems integration."

What kind of businesses will have the best chance of capturing the leadership positions in the RFID marketplace? "Vendors that seize the migration manager role," concludes The Yankee Group report, "will experience the most growth and secure the largest customer base." Vendors who act as "migration managers" are helping their customers properly implement RFID solutions, capture the right data, and use it to add value to their own products and business performance.

Companies should be busy creating business structures that enable them to work side by side with their customers to ensure that solution value is achieved. Shell Global Solutions International BV, for instance, has successfully built a high level of intimacy and value delivery into its relationship with Ferrari.

Shell is an integral member of Ferrari's Formula One racing team. Its employees wear the Ferrari Formula One uniform and travel with the team to all the Formula One (F1) races and testing sessions. They are responsible for the custom fuels and lubricants that power Ferrari's legendary F1 racers. They also conduct trackside analysis of oil and fuel samples for Ferrari's engineers before and during each race.

Even in the tightly regulated world of Formula One, Shell has been able to add value to Ferrari's efforts. In 2003, for instance, Michael Schumacher of Ferrari won his fifth Grand Prix Driver's Championship. That same year, F1 changed its regulations and eliminated refueling between qualifying and the race itself. In response, Shell Global Solutions went to work and created a fuel that both met F1 standards and gave the Ferrari team one to two more laps per tank under full power. "This is a significant advantage when planning pit-stop and race strategies," explained Ferrari team principal Jean Todt. "Ultimately there is no doubt that it has helped Schumacher win the title."[4]

The salient point here is that top business executives and market leaders should be taking the responsibility for customers' value outcomes (outcomes, by the way, for which customers willingly pay extra). They will embrace the third protocol of Prime Solutions and pursue return optimization.

THE RETURN SPECTRUM

As with the first two protocols of Prime Solutions, you can choose to approach return optimization from the three ascending levels of involvement: acquisition, installation, and results. These three levels can also be viewed as three ranges in a Return Spectrum.

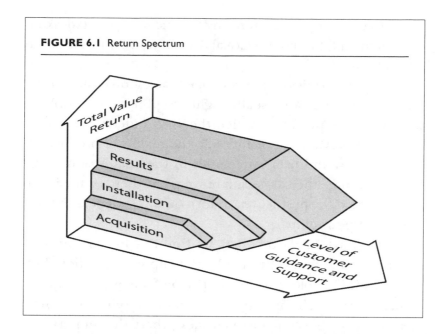

FIGURE 6.1 Return Spectrum

The Acquisition Range

In the acquisition range, sellers define value as a characteristic that is inherent in their products and the means by which those products are delivered to customers. In this context, sellers act as if their role in the customer's value achievement is complete when the product reaches the customer, even though the value is not actually achieved until the customer uses the product.

The acquisition range represents a very limited view of value accountability. Typically, this view would be seen in commodity-based markets. Office supply retailer Staples and on-line retailer Amazon.com, for example, operate successfully in the acquisition range. The value that these companies provide customers resides in the price and quality of the product—whether it is reams of paper or books. They do work hard to add value, but that work is typically focused on the ease and efficiency of the ordering, shopping, and delivery processes. Thus, Amazon and Staples built superstores and Internet storefronts that are accessible from any Internet-connected desktop computer, and they built regional distribution centers to speed order delivery.

These companies do not completely abandon customers after delivery. They are usually highly responsive to problems with defective products, which they will quickly replace or credit. But they do not venture into the realms of product implementation and use. Companies in the acquisition range might eliminate the barriers to buying, but they see the barriers to use and the postdelivery return on investment as the customer's responsibility.

Unfortunately, all too often, we find this mindset in complex markets, where the fun only starts upon acquisition. I recall a classic line told by a top salesperson for a major computer manufacturer: "This is a great job, until we sell something." What he was describing was a business where the support supplied to the customer after acquisition was relegated to damage control.

The Installation Range

In the installation range, sellers undertake the implementation of the solution and leave the customer engagement only after they ensure that the solution operates as intended. In this context, value is achieved when the solution is up and running, although customers do not actually achieve maximized value until the situation that the solution was supposed to address is resolved as promised.

Today, complex solution sellers are attempting to operate effectively in the installation range, but many are not succeeding. In fact, some solution sellers have built growing businesses around ease of installation. CRM solution seller Salesforce.com is a good example, because the company operates on a business model that is dedicated to adding value at the installation level of response.

The company offers a hosted solution in which the CRM software and databases are managed and maintained by the seller. Its solution is billed as "the end of software." Corporate buyers simply purchase access to Salesforce.com's system on a subscription basis, paying a fixed fee per user per month. By purchasing a hosted solution, customers eliminate many of the implementation costs and integration headaches of competing CRM solutions.

Salesforce.com and other companies that restrict themselves to the installation range of return optimization may be vulnerable to one fact: the successful implementation of a solution may produce value, but it does *not* ensure maximized value. One of our associates experienced just such a situation with a former employer, a large human resources training and development firm, which undertook the purchase of a state-of-the-art, high-speed digital printing solution.

The company invested months in the purchase decision. A Xerox system was chosen because its value proposition was compelling. The solution promised substantial reductions in storage and inventory costs as well as the just-in-time, in-house production of the voluminous, multicopy manuals that supported the company's training programs.

"Six months later, the purchase was made," explains our associate. "The system did exactly what the specifications said it would do—and it almost ruined the business!"

What happened? Xerox installed the new digital printing equipment, conducted training, and confirmed that it was working properly. However, it did not help the customer understand and adjust for the impact that the system would have on the existing document production process and the other established processes within the business. As a result, the equipment was not integrated with existing inventory and ordering systems. Nor was the staff prepared for the additional effort required to create and prepare new editions of documents in-house. (This work had previously been handled by their printing vendor.)

Further, the elimination of inventory created chaos in the order fulfillment process. Orders could no longer be simply picked, packed, and shipped; the documents had to be printed, too. This added a week or more to fulfillment times, a situation for which the sales force and their customers had not been prepared.

The moral of the story: Return optimization in the installation range—"It works and does what it is supposed to do"—is mandatory, but it is not enough to maximize the customer's value achievement.

The Results Range

The results range represents the highest level of return optimization. In this range, your team actively participates in the successful implementation of the solution *and* the measurement and ongoing enhancement of the results produced by the solution. In this context, value is achieved when the solution produces tangible, measurable results and those results meet the targets you promised and that the customer expects.

Prime Solutions occupy the results range of the spectrum. To achieve this level of return, you and your team must be able to do the following:

- Provide a change process—your customer must undertake change to realize performance-enhancing value—that is designed to ensure successful solution implementation and use. Depending on the complexity of the solution, this change process may include assistance in organizational change.
- Successfully define, quantify, and manage the risks along with the decisions your customer will face throughout the implementation and use of your solution.
- Collaboratively set metrics to define success levels of the implementation, and help measure and communicate

them to the customer after implementation. Strive to get everyone aligned to the change process and realization of full performance potential.

• Raise the level of value achievement by improving the solution and the return on investment to your customers moving forward.

Perhaps because of the company's heritage as a custom-order instrument builder, Waters Corporation (the Milford, Massachusetts, analytical instrumentation manufacturer introduced in Chapter 1) has naturally gravitated to the results range of the Return Spectrum. In the late 1960s and early 1970s, as a pioneer in the liquid chromatography (LC) equipment market, the young company found itself competing against industry giants such as DuPont. It met the challenge by focusing on ensuring customer results.

"We didn't always have the best instrumentation," said founder Jim Waters in a 1990 interview, "but we certainly taught chemists how to use LC better than anyone else." In fact, Waters himself personally assisted Nobel laureate Dr. Robert Woodward in his quest to synthesize vitamin B12. In 1972, when Woodward's team was struggling with the task, Waters brought an instrument to the lab and spent ten days isolating and purifying the precursor compound. The high-profile results proved to be an ideal launching pad for the LC market and the foundation for the leadership position that Waters still holds after 30 years.[5]

Waters's historical and cultural bias toward an expanded view of value accountability remains a driving force in the company. "Waters has always been one of these companies that have put a lot of value on its customers," says Peter Boler, Waters's services marketing director. "We go way out of our way to make a customer successful."[6]

In 1996, when services accounted for roughly 10 percent of revenues, the company began building a broad portfolio of services called Waters Connections. Today, Connections integrates four broad service categories—instrument and software services, regulatory compliance services, training and education, and support and information—into its industry's most diverse menu of postsales services.

Instrument and software services is the largest sector of Connections. It represents equipment warranties, service level agreements, parts, and software/hardware upgrades.

Regulatory compliance services are designed for customers who are required by law to certify equipment performance. Waters was the first in its industry to recognize its clients' needs for compliance services, and it introduced Qualification Workbooks, a standardized testing protocol for its equipment.

Training and education is the purview of Connections University. Not only does Waters provide equipment training far in excess of the usual instruction conducted during installation, it helps its clients "become better scientists" by developing and offering educational programs in the life sciences.

Finally, support and information services encompass the company's telephone and Web-based support systems. It is also the center for new initiatives such as Connections Insight, a hardware/software bundle being embedded in new equipment, which is designed to maximize uptime and performance. Equipment featuring Insight will be capable of self-diagnosis and the automatic, remote communication of maintenance issues back to the company.

One measure of Connections's success is that today, Waters' services add up to 18 percent of revenues (over $175 million per year) and is one of its fastest growing business segments. Perhaps more importantly, postsale services remain the cornerstone of the company's reputation as a leading brand in terms of value delivery. Says Boler:

> Services are a huge differentiator in how you operate, and the more differentiated you are in that regard,

the more likely it is that customers are going to stick with you. Customers are not looking for a box as much as they are looking for the solution.

AN IMPLEMENTATION PARTNERSHIP

In a 1998 working paper, which likened ERP initiatives to the creation of new business ventures, Harvard Business School professors Robert Austin and Richard Nolan vividly described the implementation challenges attached to complex solutions.[7] An ERP initiative, they said, might well cost $100 million up front and offer a potential return of $1 billion. It would also carry a 50 percent to 70 percent risk of a partial or total investment write-off and require another $200 million to avoid that write-off. Finally, the implementation team, although talented, would have an unfortunate history of missed milestones and delivery failures.

This is the description of what is obviously a high-risk venture. In fact, said Austin and Nolan, when a $5 billion manufacturing company decides to implement a $100 million ERP system, it "is an undertaking on the scale of building a medium-sized company from scratch."[8] As a result, they recommended approaching the implementation of ERP solutions as if they were new ventures and using venture capital tactics, such as the sharing of risk and reward and the staging of implementation and investment, to better manage them.

This is good advice. Complex solutions require complex implementations. Complex implementations demand difficult changes. Difficult changes create exposure to a high degree of risk. Given these conditions, it should not come as much of a surprise that solution failures often occur during the implementation process. Prime Solution providers recognize these conditions and, because failures are so costly to their customers and themselves, act as partners in implementation efforts.

As implementation partners, you can bring to the table value strategies and tactics that are informed by your broad industry experience and deep solution knowledge. These include the following.

Change Roadmaps

Although the actual implementation process for complex solutions will vary with the customer's situation, you can provide customers with a framework for approaching change. Change roadmaps may not always feature a fixed route, but they do identify the landscape that must be traversed—the starting points, interim goals, and desired ends of the implementation effort. It is critical that you also alert buyers to the barriers that are commonly encountered in the implementation process and provide strategies and tactics for successfully navigating those barriers.

In early 2004, META Group reported that the vendors who were implementing RFID to comply with Wal-Mart's mandate would receive *no* return on investment in the first two years. These early adopters are running into all the barriers inherent in an emerging solution market—"immature standards and technology, a lack of economies of scale, and limited adoption by members of the supply chain."[9]

That is not stopping forward-thinking RFID solution providers from racing to develop change roadmaps capable of yielding positive results. For example, India's Infosys Technologies, Ltd. began a number of pilot projects in the retail sector whose goal was to create "business-process blueprints" aimed at identifying the impact of RFID on retail logistics. "You have to look at RFID holistically in order to implement it successfully," Infosys chief of sales Gopal Devanahalli told *InformationWeek*.[10]

Customers need a comprehensive view of the situations and problems that could occur, so that you can work with them to mitigate the risk effectively. To cite an example of one effective risk-management strategy, we work with an IT outsourcing firm that has developed an exhaustive list of 620 items that can place the success of the outsourcing conversion at risk. This list has been compiled over 14 years and is based on the company's experiences in over 100 conversions. They have found that, in a typical conversion, 60 to 80 of the possible risk elements are present. They conduct a thorough diagnosis with each conversion to isolate those elements. As exposures are identified, the account manager walks the customer's team through each risk and determines how it will be managed.

The goal when delivering a Prime Solution is to limit your customer's exposure to risk. You should be collaborating with your customers to identify and characterize risk, analyze and prioritize it, develop risk response plans, and set plans to monitor and control it when it occurs. All of these actions increase the customer's confidence to invest.

Staging Strategies

In the Harvard study, Austin and Nolan concluded that an effective way to control the high-risk levels of a complex solution initiative, such as ERP, was to undertake both the implementation and the investment in stages. Indeed, some solution sellers are starting to create staging strategies for their offers.

Germany's SAP, for instance, built its business around enterprisewide solutions and huge implementation projects. Inevitably, correspondingly huge implementation failures have occurred, and SAP has been on the receiving end of the many negative consequences that develop when such projects go awry.

Current CEO Henning Kagermann recognized the market's reluctance to accept these large risks and the demand for an alternative. Customers, said Kagermann in early 2004, "no longer want that complete blueprint for a one-step implementation but ask for it to be broken down into manageable pieces."[11]

One of SAP's responses to this demand was the development of NetWeaver, a technology platform based on Web services that integrates people, information, and business processes. It offers an alternative to the full-blown enterprisewide implementation scheme. Once installed, NetWeaver serves as an architectural framework that allows open integration and incremental implementations.

The logic behind providing a staging strategy for complex solutions is clear. Staging makes change more manageable and success more probable. It limits risks. It requires less of an investment up front. It can also help create the kinds of short-term wins that serve as the launch pad for continued effort.

In solution markets in which the low-hanging fruit has already been picked, staging strategies serve another important purpose. They enable complex solution sellers to move down-market. For instance, the Aberdeen Group recently reported that small-sized and midsized companies want CRM solutions, but they often have a difficult time affording the investment or the risk attendant to a major implementation. "They are looking for more training, complete product sets, and vendors who can hit time and delivery objectives," said CRM practice managing director Denis Pombriant. "These smaller customers do not have the luxury of extra resources to cover a shortfall."[12]

Collaboration Tools

Open and fully transparent communication between all of the partners in a solution initiative is critical to the success of a complex initiative. The need for communication is also one of the most often underestimated, and most overlooked, prerequisites of change. Prime Solutions make a lasting and positive impact by providing the tools necessary to ensure collaboration throughout an implementation. As always, it is important that these tools are not biased toward the vendor's solution but rather toward the customer's success, and that the customer perceives them in this way.

Siemens Medical Solutions (Med) has addressed the issue of communication by becoming an early adopter of collaboration technology. A $7.5 billion health care products and services business, Med provides complex health care solutions such as magnetic resonance imaging, radiation therapy, ultrasound, patient monitoring, and information technology systems. These systems require complex implementations that involve broad-based teams made up of Med staff members and customer employees, as well as a variety of additional service providers and subcontractors.

To ensure communication, the company created the E-Logistics Virtual Information System. When a sales proposal is made, a job folder is created in the Web-based collaboration system. The system is available to all parties to the implementation. Specifications are communicated, schedules are posted, and automatic alerts can be generated to the appropriate parties.

Siemens invested less than a $1 million in the collaboration system, which is designed specifically to eliminate the problems commonly caused by missed information and miscommunications. Doug LaVigne, Med's logistics vice president, expects a six-month to nine-month payback on the investment.[13]

The communication pathways opened by collaboration also serve to keep customers close to the solution provider as the implementation unfolds. This proximity is important, because it is impossible to anticipate and eliminate every problem and hiccup that could occur in a complex solution implementation. Collaboration tools can ensure that you and your customer learn about unexpected problems as soon as possible; timing is a key ingredient in successful recovery and resolution. Timeliness and open communication also set the stage for what is perhaps the most overlooked characteristic of a successful complex solution—the measurement and enhancement of results.

RESULTS MEASUREMENT AND VALUE ENHANCEMENT

Does value exist if the customer does not recognize it? In theory, it does exist, regardless of recognition. In the real world of complex solutions, however, unrecognized value has the same negative impact on customer relationships as undelivered value. Unrecognized value can be extremely frustrating to the solutions provider, ultimately dooming the relationship with the customer. The only significant difference between the two states is how to resolve them.

Customers tend to be fully informed about solution failure; they know when their expectations have *not* been met. But they are not always so fully informed about solution success. Take CRM as an example. An Aberdeen Group research study found that about half of all CRM customers did not conduct a baseline study before undertaking an initiative.[14] This phenomenon, unfortunately, is not isolated to the software industry. We've seen it with analytical instruments, process chemicals, knowledge management, and countless others. In too many cases, no quantitative analysis of the situation happens before implementation; thus, results cannot be completely recognized afterwards. If you do not know your starting point, you cannot calculate how far you have traveled.

Solution sellers are to blame for this condition. Results measurement is the answer to the conundrum of unrecognized value, but sellers too often ignore it. A Prime Solution, in contrast, ensures that value is made tangible and is recognized by establishing realistic metrics.

Results metrics will, of course, vary with every solution and situation. Generally, however, they require selecting proper measures, establishment of a baseline, data collection, communication and interpretation of measures, and a formal review of results.

The power of results metrics can be seen in the customer relationship that IT services provider Fujitsu Transaction Solutions, Inc. has created with office supply giant Staples, Inc. In January 2000, Staples announced that it had signed a three-year service agreement with Fujitsu to provide all in-store IT systems, installation, and service for almost 1,000 locations in the United States, Canada, and Europe.

The project was valued in the tens of millions of dollars and, at that time, Staples stated that Fujitsu had won the contract largely on the basis of the value it had delivered in past contracts. For instance, Fujitsu had taken over the IT installation effort at new Staples stores and cut the time needed to complete the work in half—a key benefit when the retailer was opening a new store every 50 hours.

The service level agreement was filled with results metrics. It set unusually high service level requirements, including 98.5 percent compliance levels on professional services and 91 percent compliance on maintenance and warranty services. (Service levels are often set in the 60 percent range.) It also set targets for call response times, on-time completion of depot repair work, average spent per device, and lowered maintenance costs.

In December 2003, right on schedule, Staples announced that it was renewing and extending its contract with Fujitsu. The announcement was rife with results metrics. For instance, in three years, Fujitsu had lowered average maintenance spent per device by 60 percent, even while the number of devices grew by 20 percent annually and the number of stores grew by 15 percent annually. It had increased performance levels each contract year until, in 2003, it hit 94 percent compliance on all service-related activities, and it lowered average spent per point-of-sale terminal by 56 percent overall.

The new three-year contract is also metrics-based. Fujitsu has committed to compliance improvements and an additional 20 percent in cost reductions on key metrics.[15]

Most notable in this example is the use of metrics to define and communicate performance results and customer value. Those metrics enabled Staples to make a quality decision on its new contract. They also served as the foundation that enabled Fujitsu to enhance its value promise to Staples moving forward—the final step in the return optimization at the results level.

As the Staples service agreement illustrates, customer value is a moving target. Customer demands, competitive challenges, technological advances, and changes in the world itself all put pressure on your business to make continuous improvements in value.

Metrics can serve as the basis for that effort. As results are measured and communicated, the value cycle can begin again. Results engender questions and set off a new process of discovery. The biggest question of all is, "How can existing value be enhanced?" Companies that make an honest and energetic attempt to answer this question are in pursuit of Prime Solutions.

Datascope, based in New Jersey, is a good example of a company that recognizes the need to improve customer value continuously. Datascope is a $330 million company that manufactures products for the critical health care markets. It offers a variety of solutions in markets such as cardiac assist, patient monitoring, and collagen and vascular products. Datascope is also the pioneer in intra-aortic balloon pump and catheter technology.

As a pioneer, the company had to work hard to establish the value of its new technology. One way it accomplished value was through results measurement. In 1997, in collaboration with St. Peter's Hospital in Albany, New York, Datascope sponsored the creation of the Benchmark Counterpulsation Outcomes Registry, a database that began the rigorous, validated collection and comparison of clinical results achieved using intra-aortic balloon counterpulsation (IABC). By 1998, 132 hospitals had joined the registry, and 5,335 case records were on file. By 2000, over 15,000 case records had been collected.[16]

The registry is a valuable source of knowledge for health care professionals. Member institutions create their own databases of IABC cases and compare them to hospital averages. Patient characteristics, indications for use, and outcomes can be researched. In fact, by raising the level of knowledge regarding IABC use, it raises the quality of treatment and patient care. Don't overlook the registry's added benefit of supporting and building Datascope's cardiac assist business. It demonstrates the value of the company's products and educational capabilities, offers customers an important source of support, and starts the value enhancement cycle once more, identifying areas in which Datascope can make future improvements in its IABC solutions.

The enhancement of customer value is the key to building long-term, competitor-proof customer relationships. Acquiring a customer is not enough. With return optimization, Prime Solutions are focused on expanding business volume and retaining customers longer. The longer the customer is retained and the larger the share of the customer's business that can be earned, the more valuable the relationship. Further, the higher the value the customer achieves, the higher the barrier to change. Why would a customer leave a provider who is delivering value for another vendor whose performance results are unproven?

In the final analysis, the old proverb is sound: nothing succeeds like success. Return optimization is focused on the customer's success, and when you help buyers succeed in capturing value, you earn a multitude of rewards. Your market position, brand equity, and customer satisfaction levels rise. You enjoy deep-rooted, long-lasting customer relationships. You create profits and fuel your company's growth.

ENABLING INTERNAL AND EXTERNAL COLLABORATION

As we look to develop solutions for clients in this area, at the top of the wish list is a software tool to enable the level of collaboration we have just described in Chapters 4, 5, and 6. One of the pitfalls we encounter in clients' current software is functional biases resident in the tools. Sometimes, bias even excludes the interests of other departments, a manifestation of crossfunctional dysfunction in the tool. If the software evolves from a process that is not reflective of a Prime Solution mindset, it is only natural that the resulting tool will not reflect that mentality.

As you look to acquire or build the ideal tool, you'll want to ensure that it will guide the three major protocols we have described.

1. Diagnosing the relevant sources and uses of value you provide
2. Designing the optimal solution
3. Delivering the optimal value of the solution to your customer

Use the principles of three related disciplines and their strengths to create such a tool.

1. The diagnostic disciplines of the medical profession
2. The design disciplines of large information technology initiatives
3. The delivery disciplines of project management

The closest analogy would be a tool used in the medical profession to guide a thorough diagnosis, carry the information discovered in the diagnosis into a collaborative effort to prescribe the best care plan, and carry that care plan forward through the administration of treatment and care of the patient through recovery. The critical characteristics of the tool are that it possess complete objectivity (an ingredient painfully and obviously lacking in most ROI tools) and provide accountabilities for both the customer's team and the solution provider's team.

One of the most impressive tools we have seen was developed by Lucidus, Ltd, based in the United Kingdom. We formed a partnership with them to provide our clients with a tool that will guide the development, sales, and implementation of their Prime Solutions. Robert White, CEO of Lucidus, was one of the pioneers of IT outsourcing and was the guiding force behind Accenture's outsourcing practice. He and Barry James wrote the "book" on outsourcing.[17] After a search that included decision management software, diagnostic software, project management software, and ROI/TCO programs, the Lucidus process offered the most customer focused and unbiased approach. It was developed as an internal tool, which accounts for its lack of bias, and it covers the entire value creation and delivery process from product development through customer implementation.

Let us go on to Part Three and look at the Prime Solution Cycle for further definition of the process.

IN PURSUIT OF PRIME SOLUTIONS

The Prime Solution Cycle: An integrated value chain that unites the solution provider's R&D, marketing, sales, and service/support functions, as well as their suppliers and customers, in the customercentric and collaborative pursuit of maximized value, decision acuity, and optimized returns.

Prime Solutions emerge from a holistic approach capable of overcoming crossfunctional dysfunction, isolationism, and adversarial selling practices as well as the incomplete value accountability that so often separates businesses from their customers. In the next four chapters, we will explore how a Prime Solution evolves and enables your company to do the following:

- *Discover* and *engage* the markets and individual customers who are most likely to be experiencing the absence of the value that your company provides.
- *Diagnose* and *quantify* the problems, inefficiencies, and performance gaps experienced by your customers and stimulate their incentive to change.
- *Design* and *produce* solutions that minimize the risk of change, maximize your customers' return on investment, and provide them with the confidence to invest.
- *Deliver, measure, and improve* on the value promises that you make to your customers.

7

CREATING THE PRIME SOLUTION

If We Build It, They May Not Come

The concept of selling solutions, which has been widely embraced by today's businesses, only works if you have solutions to sell. This may seem blindingly obvious, but ironically, many of the self-proclaimed solution sellers that we meet are not actually providing solutions.

Instead, these companies are selling *as if* they were offering solutions to their customers. Typically, they are responding to competitive pressure: "Everyone else is out there selling solutions; we need to sell that way, too." They accomplish this artifice by relabeling existing products and services as "solutions" and instructing their salespeople to act as if it were so. These companies are concentrated on solution *selling,* not solution *success.*

Our firm gets hundreds of phone calls each year from senior executives of companies offering complex products and services who are confronting the consequences of this misinterpretation. They want to know why their sales cycles are increasing, why their margins on sales are being squeezed, etc.

They are wondering what is wrong with their sales organizations. What's wrong is that these companies are not offering complete solutions and so, even in the rare instances when their sales professionals are fully trained to sell solutions, they still don't have compelling solutions to sell. Thus, salespeople often resort to smoke and mirrors, which today's customers quickly see through. The end result is a high percentage of dry runs, high levels of sales activity without positive results.

Delivering solutions that offer customers maximized value, decision acuity, and an optimal return does not start with the sales function. It has to start at the beginning of the value chain, by developing a solution that encompasses those three characteristics. When we identify and track Prime Solutions back to their creation, we find some important clues as to what their development process looks like when it's working properly.

NO PROBLEM, NO SOLUTION

The frequency of new product failures is astounding. Over 60 percent of all new product development efforts never reach the market, according to Harvard Business School's Clayton Christensen and Deloitte Research's Michael Raynor. Of the remaining products, another 40 percent are not profitable and eventually disappear. The duo concludes: "By the time you add it all up, three-quarters of the money spent in product development investments results in products that do not succeed commercially."[1]

New products fail for a variety of reasons. Christensen and Raynor suggest that poorly conceived market segmentation strategies (discussed in Chapter 8) are one common cause. Another common cause, particularly in the business-to-business arena, is a flimsy or nonexistent connection to a quantifiable customer problem.

Misconnections between problems and solutions can occur throughout the value progression, but those that occur early in the development cycle tend to be lethal to solution success. Sometimes these misconnections occur because R&D is busy chasing the competition's version of the future, rushing to match the next best thing as envisioned by the competition. There is, of course, no guarantee that the competition has created a link between their solutions and actual customer problems. When that link is missing, the result is often a lemminglike, industrywide migration to solution failure.

Other times, when R&D is isolated from customers and lacks rigorous and robust customer information, it fills the void with its own assumptions about value. When this happens, the linkage between problem and solution is again subverted. This time, the solution is linked to the perspective of the internal development team, which is not necessarily an accurate reflection of the customer's perspective.

The magnitude of the losses that result in these scenarios is a function of time. The longer it takes to discover that the customer does not share the value assumptions implicit in a solution, the greater the potential loss of investment. In the worst cases, financial catastrophes, such as the Iridium bankruptcy (see Chapter 3), are the end result.

This is why Prime Solutions always begin their evolutionary development at the same basic starting point: a tangible and compelling customer problem. *There is no such thing as a solution without a problem.* Customers need not be aware of the problem that the solution addresses (that is a marketing challenge), but there must be an actual problem. To be commercially viable, solutions that sellers define as opportunities must be intimately linked to actual customer problems. A solution or, if you prefer, an opportunity without a problem is a contradiction in terms and a disaster in the making.

When solution development is examined through the filter of the customer's value drivers and performance metrics, its primary goal becomes the creation of new and better ways to solve current customer problems. It also anticipates and responds to problems that the customer will face in the future. In short, we create a source of business advantage for the customer.

The process through which these goals are accomplished is one of discovery. This discovery process is based on the need to add detail and depth to our understanding of the customer's business when identifying and solving their problems. We are seeing major solution providers restructure their offerings into industry-dedicated segments. For instance, IBM has reorganized its enterprise software around 12 industry groups. As this is written, IBM is in the process of releasing software suites that eschew the generic approach for a series of solutions, each of which is specifically tailored for the needs and problems of a vertical industry. In February 2004, IBM released software suites for banking, insurance, and financial service companies. In March, it released suites for the retail, health care, and life sciences industries. In April, software packages for the automotive, electronics, government, energy and utilities, and consumer packaged goods markets were released.[2]

These new, focused solutions are one result of IBM's "On Demand" campaign, which debuted in late 2002. In January 2003, during the company's annual worldwide management committee meeting, CEO Sam Palmisano cut off discussion about the internal resources that IBM would utilize to achieve the On Demand vision. Instead, the *New York Times* reported:

> [Palmisano] told everyone to go out and talk to customers about their most mettlesome business problems and to try to figure out how IBM might be able to help solve them. "If they got out there and actually solved the problem with the client," he said, "they would understand what we needed to do.[3]

By establishing this linkage with a customer problem as early as possible in the development process, IBM is ensuring that its solutions have the only essential form of value relevance—value on the customer's terms.

The requirement that solutions be connected to tangible problems is not an indictment of pure research. Major solution sellers around the world invest billions of dollars in research annually, much of which is only tenuously connected to current customer problems. This long-range research is typically aimed at discovering new solutions that are capable of driving future development of the markets and industries in which the sponsoring company competes.

The solutions that long-range R&D generates can be the most valuable of all for companies and their customers. For one thing, they are often unique and, thus, have no immediate competition. The exclusivity of such a solution may even be guaranteed. Patented pharmaceutical drugs, for instance, enjoy legal protection from competition for 20 years. Further, the demand for such a solution can be enormous, generating huge profits and years of growth. As with any other solution, however, the only guarantee of commercial success is having a strong link to an actual customer problem and the ability to enhance the customer's performance and success.

A BROADER CONTEXT FOR SOLUTION DEVELOPMENT

Prime Solution development requires a broader context than normal in the product development process. This context encompasses the complete consideration of the following:

- Value outcomes that the solution will generate
- Decisions that will underlie its purchase
- Challenges of implementation and usage

PARC and the Critical Connection

Xerox Corporation's Palo Alto Research Center (PARC), which was established in 1970 to discover the office of the future, is a well-known example of a world-class research initiative.[4] Leading information and physical sciences researchers were brought together at PARC and charged with creating "the architecture of information." The effort spawned a multitude of pioneering advances in personal computing, including laser printing, Ethernet, the graphical user interface, and the mouse.

One would assume that the company that virtually invented personal computing reaped huge rewards, but many of PARC's discoveries are equally well known for the poor returns that they generated for their parent company. The problem lay in the linkage between the solutions PARC was producing and Xerox's customer base. In many cases, PARC inventions were not closely related to Xerox's existing businesses, and the company was unwilling and unable to turn them into successful commercial products.

Companies such as Apple Computer and Microsoft, and new ventures formed by PARC's own researchers, reaped the rewards of Xerox's investment. For years, Xerox unsuccessfully struggled to transform PARC's output into compelling solutions. The company finally threw in the towel in January 2002, when PARC was spun off as an independent research company.

PARC's example offers many positive and negative lessons in innovation, but for our purposes there is one critical lesson: the successful commercial development of any research effort requires a direct and immediate link to your customers' businesses, their objectives, and their problems.

Too often, product development projects do not see the forest for the trees. They mistakenly focus all of their attention on a too-narrow definition of the problem. The problem is "solved" but only in a limited sense of features and benefits. Take the interrogation recording system we described in Chapter 3, for example. Confessions were being thrown out of court because of technical violations. The solution was designed to eliminate the possibility of those violations. Its features and benefits were clear—it solved the problem—yet the recording system was a commercial failure. The manufacturer fell victim to a myopic development context.

The broader context of Prime Solution development must encompass solving a problem, but in this context, the process is framed in terms of the customer's desired outcomes. In the case of the interrogation recorder, an examination of the customer's desired outcomes would have quickly revealed a serious contradiction—the desire to stop the recording and at the same time, maintain a legally sound and uninterrupted record of the proceedings. If the seller had discovered this dilemma, it might have created a solution that provided both outcomes. But even if the contradictory desires could not have been reconciled and the project had to be terminated, the early identification of the fatal dilemma would have saved the solution seller several million dollars.

A broader context also expands the development focus to include the decision process that the customer will have to undertake in purchasing the solution. For instance, we have a client who developed a product that enabled the manufacturing processes in which it was used to run more efficiently. The client's sales force is trained to place particular emphasis on the added efficiency, which also served as the justification for a premium price. There was one problem, however, that remained undiscovered until the sales force went to work: many of the company's customers do not measure and track the process parameters improved by the new products. Because customers assigned no value to the product's most important capability, their decision processes were repeatedly, abruptly, and negatively terminated.

Full consideration of the customer's decision path inevitably leads to one of two outcomes.

1. The seller may think it through, discover that a viable path to the sale exists, and proceed with the solution's development.
2. The seller may discover barriers to a positive decision (such as the inability to calculate the cost of the absence of the solution's value) and terminate or reframe the project before investing more money.

Finally, a broader context expands the development focus to include the implementation and usage of the purchased solution. As we've seen in previous chapters, implementation and usage barriers can be substantial. When companies restrict their development process to the narrow product features view, they miss the opportunity to identify and address external barriers before their customers begin colliding with them. By then, the issues still may be addressable, but it is too late to avoid solution failures, dissatisfied customers, and other negative consequences.

Clearly, an early understanding or visioning of implementation and usage factors can inform and add value to solutions. As the changes that customers must undertake to achieve a maximum return are identified, they can be incorporated into the solution or, as is often the case, added as an ancillary product or service that can generate additional value for the customer—and additional revenue and greater profit for your organization.

AN INCLUSIVE DEVELOPMENT TEAM

A sound connection to customer problems and a broader context for development are two reasons why Prime Solution development requires an inclusive solution development team.

The successful solution is built on the insights provided by a crossfunctional team, including customer representatives, a crossfunctional representation from the seller's organization, and representatives from suppliers.

Traditionally, R&D has been one of the corporate functions farthest removed from marketplace. The arrogant and outdated mindset that sellers, not their customers, drive the market was one reason for this isolation. In the late '70s, William Abernethy, a Harvard Business School professor, had done some novel work showing that something like 95 percent of all innovations were market/demand driven versus R&D driven. Clayton Christiensen's *The Innovator's Dilemma* appears to reinforce the fact that this inward focus is still quite alive and well.

Development efforts, sellers believed, did not require substantial customer input. Another reason for R&D's isolation was the security and confidentiality issues surrounding its work. The development of new products continues to be regarded as the most valuable and sensitive information inside a business. Finally, R&D's isolation was exacerbated by the crossfunctional dysfunction that often occurs in function-based organizations. Crossfunctional dysfunction occurs when internal politics and the incessant maneuvering for corporate power and resources cause managers to wall off access to their domains and restrict communication.

All of these conditions negatively impact successful solution development, which depends on open communications and broad-based inquiries. In fact, many companies are creating more inclusive development teams for just this reason.

The Customer Constituency

It has become increasingly obvious that customers are the most indispensable part of the development process, and most companies are soliciting their views and opinions. However, their role continues to be limited to traditional and less-than-robust forms of participation, such as focus groups. In November 2003, IBM CEO Palmisano explained to *USA Today* that the standard technology industry model is, "You invent, you build, you sell." But IBM, he declared, would create a new model in which, "You go out and you listen, you solve, and you craft. It's different."[5]

In IBM's model, customers must be offered a more active and integral role in issue identification and solution development. In addition to controlling the primary source of information about the problem to be solved, their cooperation is essential to understanding the decision, implementation, and usage considerations inherent to the solution. Their participation is particularly important for solutions that will require changes in existing processes and employee behavior to deliver all of their potential value.

San Diego–based Pyxis Corporation, which is creating solutions designed to streamline care delivery in health care institutions, is reaching out to its customers for information needed for a robust development process. One of its most revolutionary solutions is PatientStation SN, a computer system that resides in a pylon attached to the floor next to each hospital bed. The computer that powers the system is inside the pylon. A flat screen monitor is attached on an articulated arm, and storage drawers are attached to docking ports on the pylon.[6]

This system delivers a customized blend of information, medication, and supplies to each bedside. Patients can access the Internet, concierge service, health-related educational programming, their own records and billing, and entertainment. A Web cam allows proud parents to create live broadcasts of their newborn babies. Doctors use the system to access the patient's records, test results, and medical databases. The system allows computerized physician order entry (CPOE)—when the doctor enters a prescription, it is instantly transmitted to the hospital pharmacy. In addition, all of the supplies and medications needed by the patient are stored at nurses' fingertips.

This solution enables enormous efficiencies within hospitals, but achieving that value requires fundamental changes in established operational processes. Pyxis established a pilot program with one of its customers, Baptist Health Care South Florida. Their Baptist Hospital in Miami installed PatientStation SN at each bedside in its 51-bed Cardiovascular Step-down Unit. The pilot program's goals are to identify and address any unidentified flaws in the new solution, implementation barriers, and the changes that will be necessary in existing hospital processes to achieve the optimal return.

The Employee Constituency

The internal membership of the development team must be expanded beyond the R&D department. R&D may be best equipped to understand the capabilities of the technologies on which the solutions are based, but typically it is not the best internal source of knowledge about markets, competitors, customer decision making, and implementation and usage criteria. That is why the experts in those areas—the marketing, sales, and service/support functions, respectively—play a critical role on development teams.

IBM offers an interesting example, because it is pushing elements of the development function itself out into the field. In the past, the company typically dispatched "two in a box" (that is, a sales manager and a service employee) on customer engagements. Sales knew what solutions IBM had to offer; service evaluated the installation landscape.

With the new On Demand initiative, however, IBM has adopted a more customer-focused value mandate that requires that customized solutions linked to industry-specific problems be constructed during the sales engagement. A larger, multifunctional team is needed to understand fully the customer's situation and accomplish this task. Thus, "four in a box" is becoming the standard team size. An industry software specialist and an employee from the research lab now join sales and service in customer engagements.[7]

The Supplier Constituency

The seller's suppliers provide the final perspective essential to complex solution development. Although many solution providers continue to hold suppliers at arm's length and persist in the same kinds of price-based purchasing behaviors that they bemoan in their own customers, some companies are working hard to realize the added value that a solution-oriented supplier can contribute to the development process and the solution itself.

When suppliers are treated like collaborators instead of commodity sellers, they can contribute to solution development in several ways. For one, they can add value to the solution through the application of their own existing and emerging technological capabilities. They can also identify poorly conceived design elements before losses occur.

The Boeing Company's strategy for the design of its first new commercial jet in 14 years is an explicit acknowledgment of the critical contribution that suppliers can make in the development process. Boeing has set ambitious goals for the design and production of its new 7E7 Dreamliner.[8] The company wants to design the plane at half the cost of its last flagship plane and cut final assembly from the current standard of 13 to 17 days to just 3 days.

Boeing plans to accomplish this challenge by outsourcing 70 percent of the airplane to suppliers. To ensure that the supplier perspective is fully integrated into the design and development effort, Boeing will invest over $100 million in planning and design software created by Paris-based Dassault Systèmes and is requiring that all of its key suppliers use it, too.

Dassault's software will allow suppliers and designers located around the world to work from a single dataset, as well as simulate the lifecycle of the plane and model the impact of changes throughout the design. The Dreamliner will be the first wholly digitally designed commercial jet, and it will be the first Boeing model that relies on suppliers for this much of its design and production.

LOCATING SOLUTION OPPORTUNITIES

When we ask executives to locate the source of solution opportunities, they tend to point to R&D. This is where new solutions are expected to originate. To be fair, R&D is an important source of solution opportunities, but it's not the only one.

Apple Computer, Inc. offers a case in point. Apple is one of the world's most innovative personal computer companies. The Apple II, introduced in 1977, was the first PC to achieve market success. The Newton MessagePad introduced pen-based computing. Apple's iTunes site, introduced in 2003, is being touted as the best legal online music business. Other 2003 innovations included the first 64-bit personal computer—the fastest on the market—the Panther operating system, and a laptop designed for working in the dark.

For all of its accomplishments, Apple has continually been an underperformer in terms of market share and sales. This led *Fast Company* Bureau Chief Carleen Hawn to write, ". . . it's hard to look at Apple without wondering if innovation is all it's cracked up to be."[9]

Innovation is all that it's cracked up to be, as long as it is solidly connected to customer problems. Further, the optimal place to look for that connection is not in the research lab or design studio.

A better source of solution opportunities may well be within the customer's business. Development teams should strive to experience their solutions from the customer's point of view. They should witness how their customers decide on, install, use, and even dispose of solutions similar to those that they offer. The more we understand how the customer interacts with the solution, the more opportunity we have to create solutions that are a compelling source of competitive advantage for our customers.

The Hilti Group, Liechtenstien's largest industrial company and a global leader in construction fastening systems, created a new multimillion dollar business by examining its customers' processes for solution opportunities.[10] In 1996, Hilti sent a team to customer job sites to observe and videotape the process by which electricians fastened cable trays to floors and ceilings. The company discovered that the biggest portion of this work, accounting for 35 percent of an electrician's daily labor, was expended during the measurement process, which was done by hand. This insight induced Hilti to recruit a business partner with expertise in laser technology. The resulting laser-based measurement solution grew into a $60 million business in four years.

Japanese manufacturers have institutionalized the concept of fully examining the customer's experience for solution opportunities in a technique called *going to the GEMBA*. GEMBA, which translates as *going to the actual source*, is a unique development tool, because it is utilized before the parameters of solutions are considered. It calls for direct observation of customer behavior and personal interviews conducted where the real action occurs—where the solution will be used. The resulting information is used as the raw material for the solution development process.

Sometimes the most vibrant source of solution ideas may be with your customers' customers, another excellent hunting ground for solution opportunities.

Boeing has recognized the value of its customers' customers in the development of the Dreamliner. It has invited the general public to join its World Design Team, a virtual community whose members will provide input during the design process. Boeing will conduct surveys regarding design elements as well as early access to exterior and interior models. "You can expect to see a whole new approach to how we tell the world about the airplane and encourage participation and feedback in the work we are doing," said vice president of branding Rob Pollak.[11]

A third source of solution opportunities is in the seller's own business processes. Many sellers collect and track information for their own purposes that their customers might find very valuable. For instance, Scott Specialty Gases, a small, Philadelphia-based company that provides specialty gases to the utility and chemical industries, always tracked the cylinders holding its gases. But with the advent of the Internet, the company recognized that the cylinders also held the key to added value for customers.

"For the last three decades, we tracked the containers holding gases we sent to clients—because we rent those containers," said Leanne Merz, director of e-business. "We said, 'we have all this information about our cylinders, what's been in them, how long our clients have had them. How can this help our clients better manage their chemical inventory, and how can it help differentiate Scott from the competitors that don't have this information?'"

The result was e-Scott, launched in 1998. The portal allows customers to track their order status 24/7. It cuts customer order processing costs by 90 percent and enables customers to rightsize their gas inventory and meet EPA regulations regarding documentation and product expirations.[12]

A fourth source of solution opportunities resides in the seller's supply chain. The technologies and solutions developed by suppliers can impact the seller at the business performance level just as the seller's solutions can impact its customers at that level. In a perfect Prime Solution world, suppliers would be alerting sellers to these opportunities. But that is still an ideal world, so sellers should reach back to their suppliers to uncover those opportunities.

8

MARKETING THE PRIME SOLUTION

It's Not about Us— It's about the Customer

Companies everywhere are struggling to differentiate their offerings. They dream of establishing an unassailable market position for their solutions, a position that will enable them to capture a lion's share of the customer's mind and wallet. But to their frustration, no matter how enticingly and expertly their portraits of the solutions are painted, their solutions and their competitor's solutions usually end up looking amazingly alike to customers. Painstakingly executed solution differentiation strategies end up becoming one-way tickets to the Value Gap and painful, dry run, no-sale scenarios.

Twenty years ago, Theodore Levitt declared:

> The search for meaningful distinction is a central part of the marketing effort. If marketing is about anything, it is about achieving customer-getting distinction by differentiating what you do and how you operate. All else is derivative of that and only that.[1]

143

Sellers en masse have subscribed to Levitt's view. They first focused on the most obvious element of his distinction formula and attempted to differentiate based on the *what you do* part of the equation. They developed and marketed longer and even more esoteric lists of solution features. They also created ever more complex bundles of products and services.

This focus on solution benefits was legitimate, but two things eventually rendered it ineffective. First, the competition quickly imitated the features that proved popular with customers, so the distinction between solutions disappeared. Second, a race to add features ensued, and feature-based distinctions soon exceeded customer requirements and saturation points. When customers cannot use or recognize benefits, differentiation schemes that depend on them become meaningless.

Always in pursuit of differentiation, companies turned the focus of their differentiation efforts to the *how you operate* part of Levitt's formula for *customer-getting distinction.*

At its highest level, how you operate is represented by the business model on which your company is built. In 1996, Adrian Slywotzky, now a managing director at Mercer Management Consulting, published a compelling exploration of the power of business model innovation. In *Value Migration,* Slywotzky traced the explosive growth of companies such as Nucor, Microsoft, and EDS to their ability to create and operate new kinds of business designs that more effectively delivered value to their customers. Nucor, for instance, was able to win a leadership position in the hidebound steel industry by building highly efficient minimills that were capable of converting scrap into bar and rolled steel. In the late 1990s, the promise and potential of business model innovation also became one of the primary drivers in the rush to e-commerce. These are all examples of what Slywotzky called "a pattern of accelerating Value Migration away from increasingly outmoded business designs toward others that are better designed to maximize utility for customers and profit for the companies."[2]

New business models, if properly connected to customer problems, can be a rich source of profit. The ability to create a distinctive position in the customer's mind using the new business model is usually a longer-lived advantage than a features-based distinction. But eventually, business design-based differentiation is subject to the same problems as feature-based differentiation. Competitors adopt a similar value-delivery model, and its differentiation power fades.

By the way, your competitor doesn't have to be fully capable of delivering the new model; they only have to verbalize that capability to disrupt your differential advantage. If competitors are not content to just "me too" your capability, a race for new business designs ensues, and again, we risk outrunning both our customers' needs and their comprehension levels.

The broad concept of differentiation is not the problem here. Rather, we believe that *solution-based* differentiation is predisposed to failure. Solution-based differentiation of any kind is an Era One and Era Two marketing strategy in an Era Three environment. It is marketing that is focused on what is for sale, a subject that might engender curiosity and perhaps, a few purchases (usually among the small group of early adopters who always want the latest and greatest). However, it will not generate the level of sales necessary to establish a profitable complex solution. This is true for one final, very simple reason: *In complex products and services markets, the majority of customers do not care how "cool" your solution is.*

Business-to-business customers care about their strategies and how to execute them and their problems and how to solve them. This is why *problem-oriented* differentiation, or Diagnostic Marketing, is the most effective way to bring complex solutions to market. The goal in Diagnostic Marketing is to craft targeted messages that engage customers and move them along the progression to change.[3]

The progression to change is a spectrum, measured by physical and objective characteristics, that identifies a customer's propensity to solve a problem. It ranges from the satisfied state, in which the customer has little or no reason to change, to the crisis state, where the customer is compelled to act (which we also describe as possessing the incentive to change). Too often, marketing messages do not take this progression into account.

As individuals advance along the progression to change, they are also moving through the dimension of time, progressing from the present to the future. It is important to recognize both the physical and the mental state. They are physically in the present, which defines their reality and will, of course, be judged as positive or negative. As they consider the possibilities of changing, they will journey mentally into the future, which undoubtedly holds their greatest desires (the positive future) along with their greatest fears (the negative future).

The fundamental principle guiding behavior change is: people will not change unless the pain experienced by staying the same is greater than the pain to be experienced by changing. Their behavior and their movement through the progression to change are modeled by the psychology of change. Recognizing the tangible nature of this progression so as to craft marketing materials and message to connect with the customer precisely where they are (the proper tense) and be in sync with their progression to change creates the powerful effectiveness of Diagnostic Marketing.

SPEAKING IN THE PROPER TENSE

If you examine the marketing materials produced by most solution sellers, you will find two common threads. They tend to be focused on the solutions they offer, and they usually communicate in the wrong *tense*—a tense that speaks of a nebulous, idealized future in which the customer is enjoying the many benefits of the solution.

FIGURE 8.1 The Progression to Change

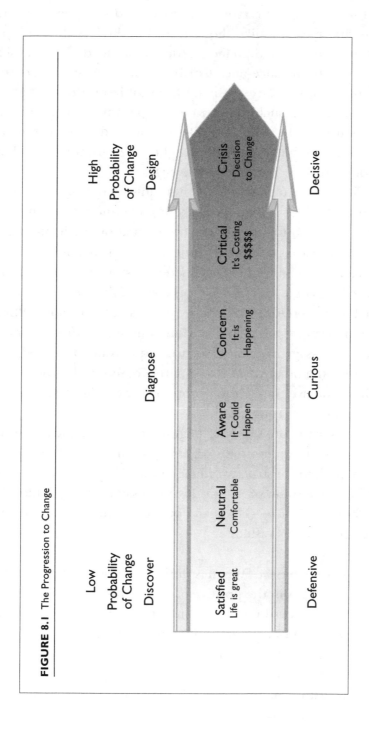

By and large, the more expensive and complex the solutions that messages like these describe, the less they compel customers to respond. In fact, if the marketing dollars that sellers spend to produce and distribute these messages produce any returns, they are typically intangible and described as goodwill assets, such as brand equity and name recognition. These are worthy assets, but like profits and loyal customers, they need not be purchased outright. They are the natural by-products of successful value delivery.

There are two fundamental prerequisites of Diagnostic Marketing. The first is that all marketing communication be centered on the customer's reality, their situation, their problems, and the physical symptoms that bring those problems to reality. You can amuse, intrigue, and interest customers with solution-focused messages, but because this communication is future oriented and therefore speculative, it is usually not compelling. Customers have grown apathetic and immune to these promise-focused messages. Symptom-focused and problem-focused messages, on the other hand, are squarely based in the customer's reality and have considerably more power to trigger serious discussion and subsequent action.

The second prerequisite suggests that, in complex markets, addressing customers in the *negative-present* tense is the most effective path to constructive engagement. This may feel counterintuitive. We think of most sales professionals as people who are "born optimists." There are four tenses in which marketing messages can be crafted.

1. *Positive-present.* When solution sellers craft marketing messages in the positive-present tense, they are describing the customer's current situation in positive terms. These messages are built around the customer's desire to sustain the current situation. This tense is only useful when communicating with an existing customer who has already achieved value using your solutions. Reinforcing

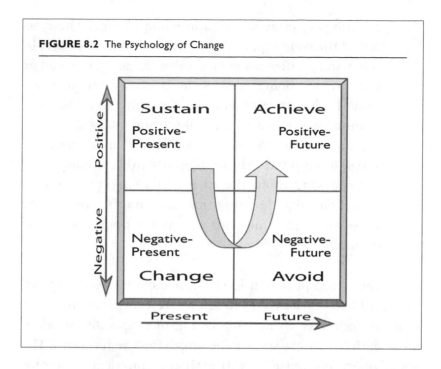

FIGURE 8.2 The Psychology of Change

the benefits of their current situation strengthens their resistance to change and fortifies your competitive position.

2. *Positive-future.* As mentioned in the opening of this section, solution sellers usually rely on the positive-future tense. These messages are built around the customer's need to create a better future. But no matter how attractive that future looks, unless the message reaches a customer who has already decided to change, it drops into the "so what?" category.

3. *Negative-future.* When sellers craft messages in the negative-future tense, they are speaking to dangers that the customer does not yet face but someday might. These gloom-and-doom messages are built on the need to avoid something that has not yet happened. Unless the future being described is unavoidable in the mind of the customer—think death and taxes—negative-future messages

are not very effective at compelling change. The reaction is the counterpart to the positive future message. In other words, the customer thinks: "It can't be as bad as they are describing," just as the positive-future message won't likely turn out that good. Customers have become immune to such messages' self-serving motives.

4. *Negative-present.* When sellers create messages that speak to customers in the negative-present tense, they are speaking about the customer's current problems and their tangible symptoms. Customers typically see these messages as no-nonsense, to the point, and highly credible.

Because complex solutions require extensive change efforts and the decisions to buy them are fundamentally decisions to undertake change, marketing messages that speak in the negative-present tense are the most effective messages. The negative-present tense taps directly into physical symptoms that the customer is experiencing at this moment. That being the case, the customer becomes engaged to determine if that symptom has undesirable consequences. The customer's desire to eliminate these consequences is the most effective incentive for change.

CRAFTING MEANINGFUL MESSAGES IN THE NEGATIVE-PRESENT

Speaking in the negative-present tense will increase the chances that a customer hears your message, but it is not always enough to compel action. For one thing, the economic stagnation that has plagued the U.S. economy since 2000 and the ensuing corporate emphasis on cost cutting have contributed to a significant rise in marketing messages that touch on the negative-present. Customers are getting more and more used to seeing them.

Secondly, the vast majority of negative-present messages are too vague to produce meaningful action. One typical example is a recent ad campaign by a major player in document management. One-third of its full-page print ad is devoted to the words *HIDDEN COSTS*. A magnifying glass over the word *costs* makes its letters appear to bulge off the page. The subhead reads: "Know what it costs to create, produce, and manage all your company's documents? Know how to cut that cost by up to 40 percent? There's a new way to look at it." The remainder of the ad is comprised of two short columns of copy that restate the subhead text and offer the reader a comprehensive analysis of the "total costs associated with all your document processes" conducted by the seller's team.

The company has the right idea with its diagnostic, negative-present approach, and admittedly, there are inherent limitations in print ads. But this ad, which appeared in *Information Week,* is ultimately too generic and too vague to compel a significant response. As a reader of this magazine, why would I think that the costs associated with my company's documents are significant? What costs might I be incurring unnecessarily? Do companies like mine incur these costs? Why would I need a new way to look at those costs? With each question, it appears more and more likely that this message is not aimed at me, and I move on.

The ad is missing *problem indicators.* Indicators bring the customer into the negative-present. They are the physical symptoms and customer profiles that provide a basis for the potential connection between the customer's reality and your solution. Indicators are the evidence that motivates individual customers to investigate a problem and, if appropriate, attempt to solve it.

The combination of negative-present tense and well-thought-out indicator connections can be surprisingly powerful. In the late 1990s, Microsoft Corporation's publishing arm, Microsoft Press, was struggling to market software-based tutorials of the company's most popular programs to personal computer manufacturers at trade shows.[4]

Microsoft's trade show presentations were focused initially on the learning effectiveness of the self-administered tutorials. In other words, they were attempting to convince PC makers to add to their costs to provide a positive-future for their customers. PC buyers, however, were not demanding preloaded tutorials, and the computer makers were already working on extremely tight margins. Typically, at a trade show presentation attended by 100 to 150 buyers, only 1 in 10 would register for a sample of the software.

The low response rates spurred Microsoft to revamp its presentation. This time, it focused on the negative-present and made liberal use of problem indicators. Microsoft did some research and quantified how much of the PC makers' customer support resources were devoted to problems related to software education. It calculated the average cost of each call and how few calls it took before the profit on a PC sale was wiped out. Then it offered the tutorials as a solution to reduce the manufacturer's cost of customer support. At the first trade show in which the new presentation was used, half of the audience came forward to obtain a sample of the software, and one major PC manufacturer signaled its readiness to begin negotiating a license to load the tutorials on each new Microsoft-enabled computer that it produced.

The Microsoft Press example gets to the heart of Diagnostic Marketing and Prime Solutions. The primary focus of both is always on customers' problems. In Prime Solution development, the provider connects those problems to the design of the solution; in Prime Solution marketing, the provider connects those problems to groups of customers or market segments.

A good rule of thumb in creating meaningful messages is always to remember that an indicator represents reality, while a benefit represents a speculative future. The better defined the indicators, the less speculative the benefit.

DIAGNOSTIC MARKET SEGMENTATION

The ad described above took a shotgun approach to the diagnosis-based marketing of solutions. It reached out to a generic corporate audience and hoped to encourage some part of that audience to identify themselves as prospective customers through self-diagnosis. But customers for complex solutions are no better at diagnosing their own problems than people who are ill. They need a resource, like a doctor, to help them understand what is wrong. What is missing in the ad is a segmentation strategy that imposes focus on the message, specifying the indicators that will enable customers to identify themselves as the message's target.

Traditionally, market segmentation has been based on demographic criteria. Some sellers split markets into geographic territories, some split them by company size, and some split them by industry classification. They also segment by product and price. Often, segmentation strategies are built on various combinations of these criteria.

Recently, new segmentation strategies have emerged that organize customers according to their value to the seller. In 2001, Hill-Rom Company, Inc., a $1.2 billion maker of patient beds and other health care equipment based in Batesville, Indiana, switched from a customer size-based segmentation strategy to a strategy based on two broad groups, *solution-oriented* and *product-oriented* customers.[5] Solution customers purchased Hill-Rom products more often and tended to buy in solution suites. Product customers tended to purchase individual products and were more price sensitive. The company found that the cost of sales to product-oriented customers was four to five times higher than solution-oriented customers. Based on this segmentation, which represented a significant improvement over size-based segmentation, the company redirected its resources and increased sales while cutting selling costs.

For all its benefits, however, there remains a crucial flaw in Hill-Rom's new segmentation: it is based on purchasing volume and customer behaviors instead of a true understanding of customers' situations and problems. As a result, customers who might well benefit from and welcome incremental solution value are seen as commodity buyers and neglected. In fact, the problem with all of the above segmentation schemes is that, in and of themselves, they do not bring solution providers any closer to that all important connection between their sources of value and their customers' actual uses of value.

To create a problem indicator-based message, solution sellers must identify a specific target audience—a group of companies that is experiencing the problems and their indicators the seller's solutions would address. To restate this in broader terms, to market a Prime Solution effectively, a nontraditional segmentation strategy based on the customer's internal profile—how they think and what they are experiencing—is needed.

Innovation experts Clayton Christensen and Michael Raynor advocate a segmentation approach that is similar in spirit to this, and they call for a fundamental revision of segmentation strategy. They say that customers "hire" products to do "jobs." Thus, they recommend that sellers segment markets based on customers' "jobs-to-be-done." In their study of successful new product development, they wrote:

> Companies that target their products at the *circumstances* in which customers find themselves, rather than at the *customers* themselves, are those that can launch predictably successful products. Put another way, the critical unit of analysis is the *circumstance* and *not the customer.*[6]

The power of indicator or circumstance-based segmentation is well illustrated by the story of Angiomax, an anticoagulant drug designed for use in coronary care.[7] Biogen, Inc. first developed Angiomax in the mid-1990s as a more effective replacement for heparin, a generic anticoagulant that had been in use since 1916 and sells for just a few dollars per dose. However, after investing $150 million and seven years in the effort, Biogen shelved Angiomax. Clinical tests proved that the new anticoagulant, which was designed for use in conjunction with angioplasty, was only slightly more effective than heparin and would require a price of $1,000 per dose to achieve an acceptable return on investment.

Enter The Medicines Company based in Parsippany, New Jersey. Medicines Co. was founded in 1996 with a unique mission: the company planned to successfully commercialize products that had been labeled failures by other drug makers—drugs that, for a variety of reasons, had been brought to late stages of development and then abandoned. Medicines Co.'s first project was Angiomax, which it bought from Biogen for an initial payment of $2 million.

Medicines Company acquired Angiomax, because it believed that there were viable markets for the drug. It went back to Biogen's test results and discovered that the drug was clearly superior to heparin when administered to patients who had suffered heart attacks two weeks or less before they underwent angioplasty. This group made up a 20 percent segment of the study, which is 10 percent of all angioplasty patients.

By focusing on this group and marketing directly to the physicians based on the group's problem indicators, The Medicines Company gained FDA approval and successfully launched the drug at a price approaching $400 per dose in 2001. In 2003, the company recorded Angiomax sales of $85 million. By 2006, some analysts are estimating annual sales of $246 million in a market estimated at $300 million annually.

DIAGNOSTIC SALES SUPPORT

A final, critical element in the successful marketing of Prime Solutions is the preparation of the tools and support materials that will be used to sell the solution. Even though the marketing and sales functions are typically seen as separate functions and are executed by dedicated departments, in the Prime Solution world, the messages through which solutions are marketed to segments *and* sold to individual customers are perfectly aligned.

Just as typically, this alignment of the marketing and sales voices is *not* seen in most companies around the world. An Aberdeen Research white paper, exploring the alignment of sales and marketing, described this problem in grim terms:

> . . . the functional relationship between marketing and sales in B-to-B markets has long been troubled. Marketing's efforts to build a consistent, compelling brand experience are frequently undermined by salespeople pressing for the next deal, whereas salespeople broadly view marketing's lead-generation efforts as ineffective and view sales collateral and support materials as off-target. Aberdeen research suggests that in many B-to-B firms, as much as 25 percent of sales reps' available selling time is spent searching for and assembling the information required for their sales calls, and as much as 70 percent of marketing's investments in sales collateral are going unused. Finally, salespeople often fail to find what they need on a timely basis, and thus—to the consternation of marketing—begin to create their own materials, with predictably uneven results.[8]

What sales collateral and support materials do salespeople need to sell Prime Solutions effectively? They need materials that can guide them through the same diagnostic approach that is used in solution development and marketing. These materials must assist them in identifying indicators and the consequences of the customer's problems that their solutions address. This is particularly important because the sales force, like many other functional groups within solution providers, is not usually thinking from the perspective of the customer's problems. Further, unlike many other functional groups, they are face to face with customers, a position where a lack of customer focus is most obvious and most harmful.

Cisco Systems, Inc. ran headlong into this problem in early 2000 when the seemingly inexhaustible market for networking products collapsed. The company's growth drivers quickly changed from products to intangible services, such as maintenance and technical support. Unfortunately, Cisco's sales strategy, a classic features and benefits approach, was not up to the job. Managers Tony Szekalski and Joshua Rossman said, "[Our] reps used the 'spray and pray' approach. Most of them would present 20 or 30 slides representing our different features and functions. But what they failed to do is understand and identify the customer's objectives."[9]

In response to poor sales results, Cisco's marketers were charged with creating new sales materials to support what Szekalski and Rossman described as "the value-selling challenge." They explained: "The value-selling challenge for our salespeople is to diagnose before they prescribe. We're teaching them to make a connection between the customer's needs and the value of products and services that lie below the surface—providing the customer with a complete picture of how Cisco can help solve their problems."

A diagnosis-based process based on Customer Message Management (CMM) principles and software powered Cisco's new approach. It was designed to assist salespeople in identifying the customer's "overall business objectives, network objectives, and associated pain points." The customer's information was aligned with seller's solutions, and together, they served as

A *Value* **T**ranslation **Q**uestionnaire

Diagnostic marketing and sales materials are constructed through a *value translation* process. This process translates the value of your solutions into terms that are relevant and compelling to customers, it targets prospects within the customer's organization, and it specifies the elements of the problem-solution connection. The seven questions that drive the process are:

1. What are your sources of value?
2. What are your customer's uses of value (the problems that your customers experience or will experience in the absence of your sources of value)?
3. What are the physical symptoms (indicators) that occur in your customer's organization that confirm their potential uses of value and validate your sources of value?
4. Where in the customer's organization are the symptoms experienced?
5. What are the consequences the customer experiences, and what is the financial impact of those consequences?
6. Who within the customer's organization cares about these consequences and their financial impact?
7. In light of the above answers, what value assumption will constructively engage the customer?

the raw material in the preparation of the presentation. Price was not discussed until the end of the sales cycle and only after customers fully understood the value Cisco was offering in relation to their problems.

The results of the new approach to sales support material have been uniformly positive. "We keep track of the customers that have gone through value-selling cycles in a best practices database," explained Rossman and Szekalski, "and so far, the accounts that have used our value approach have had a 100 percent renewal rate."

9

SELLING THE PRIME SOLUTION

*It's Not about Closing—
It's about Quality Decisions*

Take a look at most corporate marketing brochures, and you will find that they are chock full of sentiments that position the seller as customer focused and solution oriented. They portray organizations that claim to be internally united to deliver value-added solutions that address their customers' most significant business challenges. They proclaim the sellers' desire to earn the positions of "consultants" and "trusted advisors." These brochures offer an idealized, mom-and-apple-pie vision of the sellers—and what customer wouldn't want to buy from such organizations? Yet, when we poll salespeople about their roles and responsibilities, an alarming percentage still answer: "bringing in the business," "hitting my numbers," "making sales," and, of course, "closing business."

As a primary objective, closing a sale leaves a lot to be desired. A finalized sale is presumed a "win" for the seller. But in reality, whether or not a seller profits from the sale depends on its terms, the effectiveness of the implementation, and, often, the solution's performance. From the customer's perspective, a signed deal is even less noteworthy. Signing a deal provides little value to the customer in and of itself. At that point, it is an expense, an investment without return, and it is a loss if the anticipated value is not achieved.

If the sales organization's primary goal is not closing sales, what should its roles and responsibilities be? In our Diagnostic Business Development program, we suggest that one of several professions that can serve as an effective model for sales professionals is that of physician. How does a doctor respond to the question of roles and responsibilities? Doctors attempt to understand the workings of the human body and the issues and diseases that threaten an individual's health. They provide quality diagnostic services, prescribe and treat responsibly, and attempt to ensure optimal health for their patients. When we translate these responsibilities into the world of professional selling, the sales job is quite different from "hitting my numbers" and "closing sales."

The HR Chally Group, a personnel assessment and employment testing firm based in Dayton, Ohio, conducted a decade-long benchmarking study that asked customers what roles and responsibilities they wanted sales professionals to adopt. It asked "nearly 24,000 decision makers representing a broad cross-section of corporate customers" to identify what they considered the critical practices of exceptional sales professionals.[1]

One key insight revealed by the study is that customers are substantially more concerned with the effectiveness of the salesperson than they are with the solutions being offered. The top four customer responses concern the behavior and skills of salespeople. In fact, of all ten responses, six are focused on the salesperson. Responses regarding the solution, such as the quality and comprehensiveness of the solution, as well as technical support, do not appear until halfway or further down the list. The price of the solution ranks dead last in the top-ten criteria. Further and unsurprisingly, customers do not mention a

The Top Ten Practices of Exceptional Salespeople

The responses gathered during The HR Chally Group's "Customer-Selected, World-Class Sales Excellence: Ten-Year Research Report," in descending order of frequency, formed a top-ten list of world-class sales excellence competencies from the customer's perspective. They were:

1. Is responsive to needs, problems; provides service.
2. Is knowledgeable of products and customer applications.
3. Provides customer advocacy, partnership development.
4. Can keep customer up to date.
5. Provides a quality product/service.
6. Offers technical support.
7. Offers local or easily accessible representation.
8. Can provide a total solution.
9. Understands customer's business.
10. Offers competitive price.

signed sale—the ultimate goal of most sellers in the sales process—at all.

Because a Prime Solution is designed to align sales professionals and their customers in a mutually agreed objective, a signed order is *not* the appropriate goal of the sales process. The goal is a high-quality decision; that is, a sound decision based on an honest, thorough, and rational evaluation of the correlation between the customer's problem and the seller's solution. A quality decision may be a decision to buy, or it may be a decision not to take any action (not to buy).

The customer's decision not to buy is not necessarily a welcome outcome for sales professionals, but in the real world, it is a valid outcome. No matter how much salespeople would like to believe otherwise, not every customer is in a situation that requires action, and there is no such thing as a solution that's right for every situation. Therefore, the most effective sales approach is not the one that artificially prolongs a customer engagement when the solution is not required or is not an effective fit. The most productive approach is the one that "goes for the no."[2] That is, the best process facilitates the efficient diagnosis of a negative correlation between the customer's problem and seller's solution and, as quickly as possible, redeploys the team in pursuit of other possibilities.

Note that, as with the doctor/patient relationship, we do not abandon customers who are not experiencing symptoms at a level that justifies treatment. Rather, we continue to monitor their business health, to be ready to respond when appropriate.

On the other hand, all sales professionals would prefer decisions that lead to a purchase. If the decision is to purchase, it serves as an important milestone in the relationship between the customer and the solution provider, but it is not the final milestone and by no means the end of the decision process. The solution provider's journey, to create the full value of which the solution is capable, and the customer's journey to achieve that value, continue through the successful implementation of the solution. Their journeys include measuring, sustaining, and enhancing the value achieved.

To better reflect an Era Three environment and support the development and execution of decision acuity, the traditional prospect-qualify-present-close sales process requires some fundamental revisions. A better process would focus sales professionals on quality decisions, change management, and business development, instead of merely on closing deals. There is nothing wrong with closing deals, but that outcome is more effectively accomplished when sales professionals are seriously engaging customers who can achieve the highest level of value from the solutions being offered. We call this Era Three revision of the sales process Diagnostic Business Development (DBD) or, more simply, the Prime Process.[3]

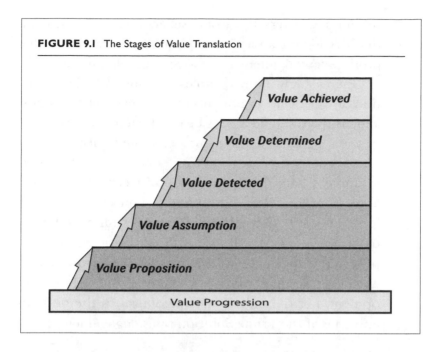

FIGURE 9.1 The Stages of Value Translation

Value Achieved

Value Determined

Value Detected

Value Assumption

Value Proposition

Value Progression

Diagnostic Business Development is a four-stage process that gives form and structure to the sales profession. It encompasses two of the fundamental cornerstones of Prime Solutions.

1. *DBD recognizes the critical importance of customers and customers' problems in the diagnostic engagement.* As we have already seen, it does not make economic, ethical, logical, or any other sense to present a solution, if the incentive to change is not established. If the problem is not understood, or if understood, a solution does not appropriately address the problem, change is unlikely. Diagnosis, not presentation, is the proper basis for the Prime Solution sales engagement.

2. *DBD recognizes that transaction-based strategies are inappropriate and ineffective in the world of complex sales.* It is a widely accepted fact that, the longer a customer relationship is maintained, the more profitable and competitor-proof it

becomes. Conversely, myopic sellers focus primarily on the individual transaction level, often not capturing the profit potential inherent in a long-term relationship.

Increasingly in the complex sale, individual transactions are critical components of long-term relationships and, as such, should always be conducted in the context of the long-term relationship. This mentality is an essential component of the Prime Solution mindset. For example, a sale that involves a multiyear service level agreement should not be approached on a transactional level. Sellers who are thinking in the simplistic terms of closing the sale will lose it to competitors who approach the engagement from broader relationship and expanded accountability perspectives. Business development, not the individual transaction, is the desired outcome of the Prime Solution sales engagement.

The DBD process encompasses the decision-making process that is required in the successful sale of Prime Solutions. Its four stages—Discover, Diagnose, Design, and Deliver—serve as a path that sales professionals can follow from the identification of customer opportunities, through the intricacies of the sales engagement, to the establishment of ongoing, long-term customer relationships.

It is worth reiterating that the ability to provide customers with and guide them through a sound decision process such as DBD is a highly valuable differentiator. In fact, we often see companies that have created profit centers around just such processes. For example, Shell Global Solutions' clients regularly contract for the firm's "opportunity confirmation process."

The core elements of Shell Global Solutions' process, in which customers will invest, are extensive diagnosis and design. Shell identifies key areas for improvement, sets measurable improvement targets, and creates a comprehensive business improvement plan. When Petrotrin (The Petroleum Company of

FIGURE 9.2 Diagnostic Business Development Process

Stage	Agenda	Value Progression	
Discover	• Prepare • Engage	Value Assumption	Premise
Diagnose	• Identify • Quantify	Value Detected	Incentive to Change
Design	• Create • Align	Value Determined	Confidence to Invest
Deliver	• Implement • Measure	Value Achieved	Results

Trinidad and Tobago Ltd) undertook this process, Wayne Bertrand, Petrotrin's operations president, said, "The Shell review process is proving an effective way of establishing an independent view of the real potential of Petrotrin's refining operations and of developing with us a realistic and practical plan to realize that potential." Petrotrin subsequently hired Shell Global Solutions to shepherd it through a five-year improvement plan.[4]

The objective, as identified during the Opportunity Confirmation Process (OCP), is to deliver net margin improvements of .70 per barrel and increase the refinery's ratings in the industry benchmarking indices. "Our objective is very clear," says Wayne Bertrand, "We need to realize a sustainable performance improvement that will keep us competitive and safe, and guarantee our future in an increasingly tough marketplace." The clarity provided by the OCP process created significant value in and of itself.

DISCOVERING THE
HIGH-PROBABILITY CUSTOMER

The first phase of selling Prime Solutions—Discover—focuses on identifying those customers with the highest probability of experiencing, or who are already experiencing, the greatest negative impact in the absence of the value provided by your solutions. These customers are also most likely to be open and willing to undertake the changes required to successfully implement and use your solutions. These high-probability customers are the most qualified prospects to purchase your solutions.

Qualified customer is an often-misunderstood term in the lexicon of complex selling. Traditionally, sellers operating in the Era One and Era Two mindset tend to define prospective customers' qualifications in terms of their demographic profiles. As with traditional segmentation schemes, these profiles are usually constructed from industry classifications, company revenue, number of employees, and other demographics. While such profiles may be useful in the preliminary identification of markets, they are much less effective in the identification of individual customers.

In DBD, sales professionals take the demographic profiles a few steps further and qualify customers within the dimensions of value. In a Prime Solution Cycle, the marketing effort provides the sales force with a value proposition. A *value proposition* is a generic statement defining the value drivers in the markets addressed by the solution, the indicators that demonstrate the absence of value, and finally, the value potential inherent in the solution. The sales force's job is to identify individual customers that fit that proposition and establish a value assumption.

A *value assumption* is an initial, informal verbal agreement between you and your prospective customer that establishes the relevancy of the decision process and provides the impetus to proceed with it. It is built on the preliminary hypothesis that the customer's business objectives are at risk in the absence of the solution that your organization provides. Customers further agree that, if the hypothesis holds true, they are willing to make the required changes to address the problem, which in all probability will mean purchasing your solution. The basis for the value assumption includes the findings of precontact research into the customer's organization and its condition, the results of a customer conversation that confirms the validity of the initial findings, and your company's ability to successfully address this type of situation.

Prime Solution sellers tend to be especially rigorous in the completion of the Discover phase. They respect the time and effort required to complete the complex sales process, and they want to ensure that customers are qualified early and often in that process.

It is worth revisiting The Graham Company at this point, because the brokerage firm offers an excellent example of this behavior. Graham's sales force contacts about 350 new business prospects each year (the companies that get beyond the precontact research). Of those companies, 90 percent are disqualified in the Discover phase of Graham's process. Vice president of sales Kevin McPoyle explains:

> When we walk in and we shake hands and we exchange cards, we are not asking people for an opportunity to quote. We want to hear about the organization and its risk issues. So I would say that what is different is that we discuss and listen before we offer.
>
> We listen for that pain, and we listen for the clues that we think verify our value proposition. When they are done and we have asked about their expectations and their decision process, we'll spend a few minutes talking about what we do.
>
> We are walking out of that first meeting with permission to conduct a thorough risk-management assess-

ment so we can help the customer quantify the pain. That being said, we recognize that this approach is not for every customer. We try not to judge people's decision-making process, but if it doesn't fit, it doesn't fit, and that's okay. We have other things to do.[5]

Graham's risk assessment requires that their team of professionals be given total access to the customer's business and staff. Many prospective customers balk at that requirement, but Graham is adamant about the necessity of a sound decision process and will not proceed with any sales engagement that must depend on a less-than-robust process.

Graham's willingness to disqualify a prospect when access is limited and/or the value assumption cannot be verified represents a classic Era Three behavior. In Era Three, effective salespeople are perceived as professionals and the relationship with the customer is governed by mutual respect. An integral element of that respect is the agreement to progress as partners through a sales engagement that is based on value.

DIAGNOSING COMPLEX PROBLEMS— CREATING THE INCENTIVE TO CHANGE

The mutual acceptance of a value assumption is the foundation for the Diagnose phase of DBD. The process of diagnosis is one of *hyperqualification*—in essence, this work is a continuation of the customer qualification process in greater detail and depth. During hyperqualification, the full extent of the customer's problem is explored, measured, evaluated, and communicated. This phase's goal is to raise customers' awareness of the problems they are experiencing.

Diagnosis is only half-heartedly incorporated into most selling processes, and it is rarely professionally executed. Most often—and this is particularly true of needs analysis—the seller allows and sometimes encourages the customer to self-diagnose its problems. In Chapter 8, we saw that the belief that customers can self-diagnose their problems can often lead to ineffective marketing materials; in the sales process, the shortcomings of self-diagnosis are compounded.

It is only natural that customers will want to and will begin to self-diagnose. This behavior is to be expected and respected, but not accepted. To put it bluntly, self-diagnosis is one of the most significant contributors to the Value Gap. Here are four reasons why.

1. *Customers often misdiagnose their problems before and during the sales process.* It is only natural, when recognizing an issue or concern, to begin to figure out how to address it. When salespeople conduct a traditional needs analysis, they are accepting this self-diagnosis along with the customer's self-prescription. When that happens, the seller will often prescribe the wrong solution, which, in turn, leads to solution failure with all the attendant negative consequences.

2. *Self-diagnosis represents a missed opportunity for sellers to demonstrate their knowledge and expertise by taking the diagnosis to depths the customer would never have considered.* This is a tremendous missed opportunity to differentiate themselves and their solutions from the competition. It forces sellers to depend on solution-based presentations, which all sound alike to customers.

3. *Self-diagnosis represents a missed opportunity for customers to get an outside view from professionals.* Experienced, Era Three sales professionals have likely seen and dealt with similar circumstances of pain and problems at other firms.

4. *Because self-diagnosis is often a less-than-comprehensive process, the total cost of the problem is not established.* Thus, the

seller's ability to construct a compelling business case for the solution is seriously restricted.

Sun Microsystems has taken these lessons to heart in its education and research business unit.[6] In the past, explained U.S. education and research director Joe Hartley, when a customer contacted the group in search of a storage solution, the salesperson would ask the customer how much storage was needed. Then, a proposal and a price based on the customer's answer would be produced and presented. The result? "We might propose the wrong solution," said Hartley, "or potentially miss out on a larger opportunity where what [the customer] really needed was a combination storage service and tape-drive system."

The Sun group used collaboration software to build diagnosis into the sales process. It now uses a relationship management suite created by Knowledge-Advantage, Inc., based in Hummelstown, Pennsylvania. This suite enables Sun's 100-member field representative team and its customers to identify and share the parameters of the problem and create a solution that is based on the customer's requirements.

Interestingly, when the Diagnose phase of DBD is properly executed, customers most often make the decision to change during this phase, and, thus, they decide to buy complex solutions. A properly executed diagnosis detects the absence of value, maximizing the customer's awareness of the risks of their current situation and the need to resolve it. Neither glitzy presentations nor high-pressure closes can accomplish this result on their own. In fact, those techniques often delay the result or even lead to failure.

The actual work of diagnosis is a combination of symptom identification, fact finding, estimation, and prioritization. Symptom identification and fact finding require that a full of cast of characters (see Chapter 5)—the people within the customer's company who provide access to key information needed to complete the decision process—be identified and a question-driven process be used to elicit that information. Estimation is the process of assigning a total cost to the problem. Prioritization is the evaluation process by which that cost is weighed in light of the customer's business goals. When all of these tasks are completed, so is the Diagnose phase of DBD.

In value terms, the Diagnose phase is complete when value has been detected, the physical symptoms are verified, and your team and your customer reach a verbal value agreement about the dimensions of the problem. Like the value assumption, the *value agreement* is an informal statement specifying the scope of the customer's problem. More importantly, it serves as mutual agreement regarding the cost of the problem and how it is prioritized in the customer's business. This, in turn, justifies the continuation of the decision process to the Design phase of DBD. Your customer has clearly established the incentive to change.

By the conclusion of the Diagnose phase, your team will have established exceptional credibility with your customers. Your ability to understand the customer's business (which was identified as a top-ten sales practice in Chally's study) and identify the sources and intensity of customer problems often places your company on an inside track to the final decision. This is a track of competitive advantage on which less-astute solution sellers will have great difficulty maintaining the pace.

In fact, our research has shown that when the Diagnostic process is employed, most likely by the conclusion of the Diagnosis, the customer has decided to change and has decided to use the professionals that guided the diagnosis to provide the solution. The credibility built by your team during the diagnosis transfers to your solution recommendation. The customer's logic is: "If they understand the problem that comprehensively, they must have a solution that will be equally comprehensive." It is a fascinating and effective competitive strategy. Differentiating during the Diagnosis provides a preemptive competitive positioning that is difficult, if not impossible, to dislodge.

DESIGNING OPTIMAL SOLUTIONS—CREATING THE CONFIDENCE TO INVEST

The Design phase of DBD is all about solutions, but it is *not* about *your* solutions. The goal of Design is to define the parameters of a high-quality solution in reference to the customer's problem. It identifies the *optimal solution* as a series of product and/or service parameters that are designed to minimize the customer's risk of change and maximize the value to be achieved. Toward this end, your team will work to identify and confirm the customer's desired outcomes and how best to achieve them, but it will not formally present your company's solutions.

Most sales processes do not work this way. Typically, after needs are assessed (this can be very superficial), sellers move directly into presentations that are focused almost solely on the solutions offered by their companies and the positive characteristics of their company. When sellers do this, they neglect to establish the critical connection between the problem and the solution in the customers' minds. As a result, customers have a difficult time distinguishing between unique competing solutions, and the outcome of the sale becomes randomized.

Instead, sellers of Prime Solutions use the Design phase to focus the customer's search on the best solution. Again, The Graham Company provides a good example.[7] When Graham completes a thorough survey of the risk issues and history of prospective clients, it does not simply prepare a quote. Instead, the company specifies the structure of a portfolio of coverage that is capable of addressing and managing the existing risks. The goal of this work is to ensure that, when customers make the final decision, they will be able to evaluate alternative proposals in relation to coverage needs as opposed to the bottom line price. This enables customers to avoid a situation that Graham's vice president of sales, Kevin McPoyle, likens to "buying a life insurance policy with a death exclusion. It seems to be a great deal . . . until you make a claim."

Establishing critical solution criteria *before* presenting the solution itself allows your team to address the ramifications of competing solutions from a criteria perspective. All too often, solution sellers deal with competitors' solutions by either acting as if they do not exist at all or attempting to denigrate them. Both responses are unproductive: the former suggests that the seller does not know the market; the latter suggests that the seller is unprofessional. When your team discusses and assists your customers in establishing design and selection criteria, both negative responses are avoided, and often the criteria set itself enables the customer to eliminate your competitors.

In Design, your company has the opportunity to address competing alternatives head-on. The willingness to do this reinforces the cooperative partnership between your team and your customer's team. It also enables your team to reinforce their position; they can ensure that the customer properly recognizes and weighs the inherent value advantages of a design that matches your solutions.

The Design phase is aimed at establishing the decision criteria that will be used in the evaluation of solutions and their providers. Your team assists your customer in the quest to understand their desired outcomes, the value of those outcomes, and the timing in which the value must be delivered.

In value terms, the Design phase of DBD is completed when your team and your customer establish the second half of the verbal value agreement, which specifies the dimensions of the solution. Another informal statement, the *value agreement* defines the customer's solution expectations and the criteria that will determine the solution's features. It also serves as the basis for the *discussion document,* a written statement that confirms the findings of the decision process thus far and ensures that your team and your customer are in accord (have established a mutual understanding) regarding the significance of those findings.

A discussion document is crafted with the customer. It is a working draft that provides the foundation on which a formal proposal can be constructed. When your customer signs off on the discussion document, you are assured that your collaborative approach and guidance has created the foundation for a solid proposal based on sound reasoning and accepted fact. When a customer will not confirm the document, it is invariably a signal that the decision's foundation is flawed and that your team must identify the customer's issues and resolve them before moving forward. It is a final sanity check before proceeding to proposal.

By the conclusion of the Design phase, your team has demonstrated its integrity to your customers. It has created a solution framework based on mutually agreed-upon facts. Your customer will have established the confidence to invest.

Once again, it bears repeating that Prime Solution sellers always recognize that there may not be a fit and are continually "going for the no." If, at any point in the Diagnostic Business Development process, you discover that your solutions do not properly serve the customer, your team would so advise the customer and suggest the engagement be postponed or ended with integrity.

PREPARING FOR PRIME SOLUTION DELIVERY

In the Deliver phase of DBD, the work of previous phases is encapsulated in a formal proposal. The result is a proposal that is fully informed by the customer's problem, the customer's expectations for a solution, and the solution recommendation—a recommendation that is focused on and tightly aligned to the customer's requirements.

The DBD proposal stands out in sharp relief when measured against the typical solution proposal. For one thing, the DBD proposal does not overemphasize the solution. It is a balanced presentation that includes a complete and relevant portrayal of the decision process. For another, the features and cost of the solution in the DBD proposal are counterweighted by the realities of the indicators and the costs of the customer's problem (the documentation of the customer's incentive to change). The customer can clearly evaluate the solution in business and financial terms.

Most importantly, there are *no surprises* in the DBD proposal. The proposal that emerges from the DBD process is a *confirmation* document. Customers have already confirmed almost everything in this proposal. They have confirmed the dimensions of the problem and their expectations for the solution. As long as the solution proposed meets these specifications, there are no questions and no objections. The actual closing process is usually a foregone conclusion and an anticlimactic formality.

This stands in stark contrast to the typical proposal, which is predominately focused on the seller's organization and their solutions. With the content of the proposal focused on the solution and its features and benefits, customers are forced to justify for themselves whether the solution is a sensible investment. Finally, in this form, the typical proposal is an instrument of *consideration*–literally meaning a suggestion or recommendation. Seen as a consideration, it actually invites additional scrutiny. Because this is often the first time the customer may be considering some of the proposal's elements, if it does not answer all of the customer's concerns, objections are raised. Each objection restarts the sales process, prolonging the sales cycle and delaying the final decision, which remains at risk.

The work in the Delivery phase of DBD encompasses reviewing the formal proposal and the customer's official acceptance of your solution. It also extends to the preparation for and implementation of the solution.

Part and parcel of the foundation of the Delivery phase are the Design conversations that included the frank acknowledgement that bad things can happen to good projects, no matter what. The honest assessment of solution implementation and usage challenges is a prerequisite in the Era Three level of professional selling. Not only is this an ethical sales practice, but customers are increasingly demanding it.

We came face-to-face with the consequences of this demand a few years ago while interviewing customers for a client company. We asked a CIO who had spearheaded a $6 million purchase from our client about the key factors in his company's decision process. He replied:

> This purchase involved a major change for us. But when I asked "Vendor A" what sort of problems we could expect with an implementation of this nature, they claimed that there really shouldn't be any problems at all. "We do this all the time," they said. "We have systems and methods in place to ensure a worry-free implementation."
>
> Fundamentally, I eliminated that vendor at that moment. Anyone who could say this was not going to be problematic was either clueless or assumed I was. Either answer won't cut it. I am living through my third conversion, so you don't tell me there won't be any problems. I've got scars from every one of them.
>
> When I asked that same question of [our client's salesperson], he said, "I have got to tell you that this is probably going to be on a degree of difficulty comparable with the most complex implementation you can attempt. There is hardware, software, and multiple operational processes involved. We have built the systems to anticipate and to navigate through that change, but

despite all of that, there are going to be things that none of us could have anticipated." When I think back, that's when I started thinking, "These guys have their feet on the ground."[8]

In value terms, the completion of the Design phase signals the start of solution implementation and tangible *value achievement*. By the conclusion of the Design phase, your company has established exceptional credibility with your customers. Now your team must deliver on value promises.

10

DELIVERING ON THE VALUE PROMISE

Promising Value Is Expected— Delivering Value Is Exceptional

The final phase of the Prime Solution Cycle is often the most problematic for solution sellers. This is the phase of value promise delivery, also called value release, and it encompasses solution implementation, reporting results, and ongoing enhancement of returns. These can all be centers of high potential profit for both you and your customers. Conversely, when poorly executed, they can just as easily become centers of significant loss in both financial and relationship capital.

The salient issue here is successfully transforming the solution's value potential into tangible customer results. A company's acceptance of accountability for this transformation and its team's ability to facilitate it are critical to its long-term success. Michael Cusumano, MIT Sloan School of Management professor and a leading authority on the software industry, identifies the capability to deliver on value promises as a key ingredient in the establishment of credibility in the market-place. In his latest book, *The Business of Software,* he says:

> Loss of credibility can be fatal for enterprise software companies because they, especially, need to maintain a position of trust with their customers and stakeholders. Problems rarely require the kinds of maneuvers that Enron, WorldCom, or Tyco International employed in the early 2000s; they are usually more straightforward and subtle.
>
> For example, do you deliver products and services to customers based on what you said you would do and more or less on the schedule you promised? Well-managed companies try to do their best to make good on their promises, even if they lose money in the process. Poorly managed companies try to "get the business" at almost any cost and cut corners on what they deliver or deliver late because they know they overpromised to make the deal.[1]

Whether promises are intentionally or unintentionally broken, the consequences can be severe. Consider, i2 Technologies, Inc., the supply-chain management software company that Nike blamed for its quarterly results shortfall (see Chapter 1). In 2002, in an effort to establish the ROI of i2's solutions, Nucleus Research, Inc. contacted the customers who were featured in the success stories on i2's corporate Web site. The study found that "55 percent of i2 customers interviewed did not believe that they had achieved a positive ROI from their deployments after having used i2 for an average of 2.2 years." Further, nearly 70 percent of the i2 implementations lasted an average of three times longer than initially planned; the ROI estimates, which had been calculated during the sales process and on which the solution pricing was based, often proved to be exaggerated; and, according to customers, i2's services staff and outside consultants, lacking expertise in the software, were unable to solve "problems inherent in early versions of i2 software" and were inexperienced at aligning i2 solutions with existing customer processes.[2]

As customers struggled to achieve the value, i2's high-flying stock plummeted (along with the market at large) from $111 in 2000 to 41 cents in 2002. (As this is being written, it is still under $1.) In 2002, the company reported a loss approaching $8 billion on under $1 billion in revenue. According to MIT's Cusumano, who consulted with the company as it tried to right itself, i2's solutions did have value potential, but implementations were often botched.[3]

While sellers who miss their goals suffer, those who successfully deliver on their value promises earn returns that are sometimes out of proportion to their actual achievements. IBM, as we have already seen, is aggressively building its value delivery capabilities. In a 2004 ERP brand research study conducted by The Yankee Group, respondents cited IBM "more favorably on desired attributes than well-known category players such as Oracle and SAP."[4] Actually, IBM was ranked as the brand with the highest differentiation score among a field of ten ERP vendors. This ranking is in spite of the fact that IBM does not offer its own ERP software. The Yankee Group's logical conclusion: "IBM should exploit its impressive ERP market strength."

The logical conclusion for business-to-business sellers is this: *a solution that does not deliver value as promised is no solution at all.*

CHANGE MANAGEMENT DRIVES IMPLEMENTATION SUCCESS

Complex solution implementations typically require that customers undertake major changes in their businesses to achieve the highest degree of value. The ROI of enterprise-level solutions, such as ERP, is based on the assumption of fundamental change. Another example is RFID, whose broader value promise is based on a radical change in quality and depth of product tracking information and the customer's ability to respond to that data. More dedicated solutions, such as CRM software for call centers, sales force automation, manufacturing control systems, and sophisticated medical equipment, also require fundamental changes in operational processes and adjustments in the larger systems that intersect them. For all of these reasons and more, your ability to manage and facilitate change *is* the core competency in Prime Solution implementation.

In a Prime Solution environment, successful organizations accept accountability for guiding and ensuring the success of the changes that customers must make throughout the solution cycle. In the development phase, they are considering ease of implementation in solution design. In marketing and sales, they are diagnosing the degree of change needed and the customer's receptiveness to change. In the service/support phase of the Prime Solution Cycle, sellers are, at the very least, serving as change navigators or change enablers for their customers.

As change navigators, solution providers bring customers a process that can carry them from their current state to the future state promised by the solution. An effective change management process is an essential ingredient of the Prime Solution. A detailed treatise on change management is outside the scope of this book.[5] I'd like to refer you to the seminal work of John Kotter. In his book *Leading Change*[6] he points out that even when the need for change is compelling, needed change can stall because of inwardly focused cultures, paralyzing bureaucracy, parochial politics, a low level of trust, lack of teamwork, arrogant attitudes, a lack of leadership in middle management, and the general human fear of the unknown.

John goes on to introduce an eight-stage change process designed to address the eight fundamental errors that undermine change efforts.

1. Establishing a sense of urgency
2. Creating the guiding coalition
3. Developing a vision and strategy
4. Communicating the change vision
5. Empowering broad-based action
6. Generating short-term wins
7. Consolidating gains and producing more change
8. Anchoring new approaches in the culture

Missing any one of these stages will undoubtedly contribute to a Value Gap. How well does your implementation support plans ensure that your customer can adequately fulfill these eight stages?

Supporting the customer's change process as they embark to implement your solution is perhaps one of the most critical capabilities and undoubtedly contains the potential for compelling differentiation. It is important to note that all successful change management processes must fulfill two conditions: It must be adaptable and it must account for three primary elements: technology, process, and people.

Adaptability

A fixed, one-size-fits-all approach to complex solution implementations is simply not effective.

Every solution implementation is conducted in a unique environment. This is particularly obvious when a seller's solutions are aimed at a wide variety of industries. The data storage needs of a manufacturer will clearly be different than the those of a retailer. However, the need for flexibility becomes less obvious as solutions become more focused (a trend that is currently emerging). It is easy to forget that every company has a unique culture that mysteriously governs the behavior and responses of the people who will use the solution. Each company within an industry also contains a unique blend of systems and processes. Compounding the problem is the fact that unique environments extend to the business units of individual companies. Different divisions of global corporations, especially those that have been cobbled together through mergers and acquisitions, will often feature differences as pronounced as those found between different companies.

The implementation/change process must respond to differences between customers as well as within them. The process must be able to assess existing systems and design customized strategies for change, before you embark on the implementation process. It must be capable of soliciting customer input and transforming that input into process terms. As described in Chapter 6, it may also mandate the use of pilot programs and staged implementations to test the proposed strategy's and build customer confidence.

Technology, Process, and People

The change process must consider and account for three primary elements: technology, process, and people. When the solution itself is value capable and a quality decision has been made, solution implementation failures can usually be tracked to one or more of these elements.

Technology. Often, sellers approach the installation of their solutions as if they were working in a vacuum. This mistake is elementary and a classic implementation failure scenario. Nonetheless, it remains common, particularly in the high-tech hardware and software industries, where horror stories detailing the consequences of technological incompatibilities abound.

The demand for the smooth integration of technology is so great, it has spawned an entire industry devoted to the creation of middleware. *Middleware* is the software that serves as the glue between applications and networks. Much of it is designed to facilitate and accelerate system integration, such as enabling front-end CRM applications to access customer data that is already resident in dedicated, legacy databases.

At the first level of change consideration, solution implementations must be successfully integrated with customers' existing technological infrastructures. Virtually every customer has existing platforms and systems. Even new companies in their start-up stages typically purchase solutions from multiple vendors, all of which must be integrated before implementation can succeed.

Thus, the change management process cannot be conducted in a vacuum. It must identify potential technology conflicts, resolve them before installation, test to ensure compatibility, and plan for unexpected problems. In short, sellers must be able to plug in their solutions without disrupting the customer's existing technology.

Process. Solution compatibility issues extend from technology to processes. When sellers implement solutions without considering their impact on the customer's existing business processes, they are courting implementation failure. At a recent industry conference, John Chambers, CEO of Cisco, outlined the impact of recent productivity improvement initiatives that revolved around applying new technologies to support business processes. They found that applying new technology along with improving the underlying business process produced a four to five times improvement over applying the technology only. He cited the example of CRM. If you just install CRM, you might be looking at a 6 to 9 percent productivity improvement. If you work to reengineer the sales process itself, you will be looking at a 25 to 30 percent improvement.

Typically, solution sellers do consider the primary process impact of their solutions. An RFID vendor, for example, will almost certainly understand the changes that its solutions create in existing warehousing processes, such as receiving. But the secondary and tertiary process impacts are less often fully considered. For example, the data generated in receiving is used by a variety of other processes, such as accounts payable in the reconciliation of purchase orders and payment generation, and manufacturing in its scheduling and forecasting.

At the second level of change consideration, the impact of solutions on existing business processes is examined and aligned. In most cases, new intersections between processes will have to be crafted; in some, multiple processes will have to be reengineered.

As with technology, the change management process cannot operate in a vacuum with regard to processes. It must identify the processes that the solution will affect, both upstream and downstream, and redesign the workflow as needed to ensure a smooth implementation.

People. The human factor in solution implementation is notorious for its ability to derail change, devalue solution investments, and widen the Value Gap. Further, people issues tend to be among the most often neglected by solution providers.

Here's how Sumantra Sengupta, CIO of The Scotts Company, the leading seller of lawn and garden products, weighs the human factor in complex solution implementations:

> The correct strategy, coupled with a robust process design and a scalable technology platform, will lead to successful business transformation. But it will deliver zero value to the business if we don't have the right people with the right mix of skills and abilities assigned to the right roles, and if we fail to motivate them by using the proper metrics.[7]

In 2003, when Scotts undertook Project Pegasus, a major initiative aimed at uniting the disparate local information systems and the four separate transaction systems in its European business units into a single system, Sengupta paid particular attention to the human factors. He found that resistance to change stems "from three major sources: skill-set alignment, focus, and attitude."[8] He made sure all three issues were addressed in the successful seven-month conversion effort.

At the third and most critical level of change consideration, solution providers must identify and address the human factor—the impact of their solutions on people. To ensure successful implementations, your company must understand that technology and process changes are rarely transparent; these changes almost always directly or indirectly affect the people who operate the technology and processes and/or depend on their output. Your company must also realize that, while the logic and beauty of your solutions may appear compelling from your perspective, they are not self-evident to those people whose routines are permanently disrupted.

Complex solution implementations invariably involve people. Thus, an effective change management process must identify and provide the physical skills and the behavioral and belief sets that are required to accept and utilize the solution.

THE UNCEASING DEMAND FOR VALUE ENHANCEMENT

For all of their complexity, the business-to-business whole solution markets would be simpler environments in which to prosper if a successful implementation marked the end of the value chain, but this is not the case. The value chain is more accurately described as a *value cycle*.

To capture the complete value, you must approach value achievement as a progressive cycle. Value is not a fixed target.

The Value in Change Management

The ability of your entire organization to help customers navigate the change required to implement the solution is a prerequisite for your success, but today, it is more akin to the game's ante than a winning wager. Some companies today are willing to go to greater lengths than ever to ensure customer success.

Georgia-Pacific Resins, Inc. provides a good example. The adhesives that the company develops for composite panel manufacturers can be treated as commodities. But the GPRI has long known that the knowledge of the production process that is resident within the company has much broader applications for customers. Dan DiCarlo, GPRI's adhesives group business manager, explains:

> The perspective we like to choose, and it is probably a little bit more difficult to sell, is what we have to deliver is not always tied to the adhesive. It's the knowledge and the technical aptitude that our customer gets as part of the G-P solution. It's a combination of product, process, and performance. The performance comes through technical expertise in developing the right products for our customer's application, as well as helping them put systems in place that allow them to achieve better process management.

GPRI delivered this added value to one customer, a leading panel board manufacturer, as it undertook the start-up of a new plant. Instead of simply quoting a competitive price for its adhesives, GPRI offered to take an active, consultative role that spanned the design through start-up phases. Based upon the customer's assessment of the value of such start-up assistance and support, GPRI was awarded the initial resin supply for the plant. GPRI assisted in selecting manufacturing equipment, created process training manuals that the customer still uses to educate new hires, developed lab protocol for quality control and regulatory compliance procedures, and assisted in the data collection and interpretation systems that enable prompt and accurate process control in real time. Says DiCarlo:

Our people were in this plant so extensively and for such a long period of time, for months during the start-up period, that, in effect, they became an extension of the operating management people of the plant.

The customer found the value that GPRI was able to deliver in its change effort so compelling, it did not seriously consider any of GPRI's competitors when this customer started up a second facility sometime later.

First, it moves according to your company's internal growth requirements. Your stakeholders demand growth, and the only way to provide it is to provide enhanced value promises. Second, the value target also moves in response to external competitive pressures. Your competitors will drive value enhancement through their own quest for advantage in the marketplace. Third and most compellingly, customer demands propel the value target. It is not enough to offer even the most comprehensive solution. To maintain and retain customer relationships, you must offer customers continually enhanced value achievement opportunities.

The growing customer demand for enhanced value is particularly visible in complex solution markets, such as business process outsourcing services. In the past, the primary value promise of outsourcing was cost reduction. Sellers were saying that they could run the customer's business functions or processes at less cost than the customer could; therefore, it would cost the customer less to turn over the reins to the seller.

In the current environment, however, customers seeking a quality outsourcing solution cannot afford to be satisfied with cost savings alone. They must also achieve the added value that comes from process improvement. This expanded role for business process outsourcing has given rise to the concept of "business transformation outsourcing."

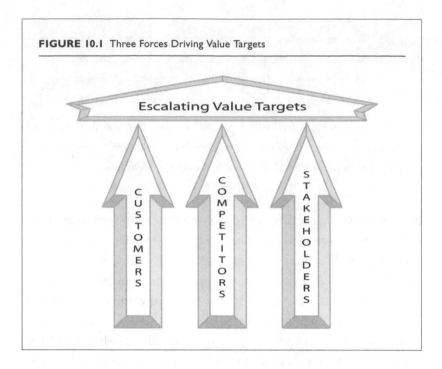

FIGURE 10.1 Three Forces Driving Value Targets

The relationship between Blue Cross Blue Shield of Massachusetts (BCBS) and Electronic Data Systems Corporation (EDS) provides a good example of how this trend is playing out. BCBS has outsourced its computing processes to EDS for 34 years, and in January 2003, the companies announced the signing of a new ten-year, $320 million outsourcing services agreement.

The new agreement, however, covers more than the outsourcing of existing operations. It commits EDS to "help us deliver value to our customers so that we maintain our business competitiveness," according to Carl Ascenzo, BCBS's CIO. Toward that end, EDS will create an enterprise system based on its MetaVance health care software, which will enable BCBS to offer its member-customers greater access to their accounts and benefits information. Ascenzo told *InformationWeek:* "Outsourcing relationships are becoming more about strategic partnering, and as we go forward, we need to align with someone who brings not just computing scale but who understands our business."[9]

For customers, the continued enhancement of value is an obvious and compelling distinction between the average vendor and a strategic partner. Motive, Inc., the service management software company introduced in Chapter 1, has always taken an intense interest in expanding its customers' value achievement.[10]

The company's earliest acts pegged it as a Prime Solution provider. Before Motive employees wrote a single line of code, they conducted studies at 30 customer service centers and IT support centers. Using time-and-motion techniques, Motive identified exactly what happened when their future customers' customers called with tough problems, and it documented the resulting waste. Based on this information, the company developed automated service software solutions that enabled its customers, including cable companies, Internet providers, PC makers, and warranty service contractors, to capture substantial cost-of-service savings.

Even in the few years since its 1997 founding, Motive has demonstrated an intense drive to enhance the value of its solutions. For example, in 1999, it established a business unit called Leveraged Marketing, later renamed Collaborative Marketing (CM). The sole purpose of CM is to help Motive's customers leverage the value of its solution. Motive cofounder and chief marketing officer Mike Maples explains:

> We recognized that some of our customers would be more successful if they found ways to market our capabilities to their downstream customers. For example, if [a customer] is coming out with an activation capability for broadband access, if the user interface is easier for the end subscriber to use, more activations will occur and less service truck rolls will occur.

So, as a company we had to decide, do we want to just say, "Okay customer, here is our software. It does what it says it will do. Go knock yourself out." Or, did we want to say, "Okay, we are really not selling software; we are selling an outcome." Selling an outcome would mean that we need to develop an expertise in collaborating with our customer to help them think through [their customer's usage] issues . . . how little things could mean a lot in terms of causing adoption rates to accelerate and truck rolls to decline rapidly. So we have people in Motive who don't have a quota, who get no revenue credit, who don't do any deployment services. All they do is collaborate with our customers' marketing people to ensure that the enablement and adoption of our software is maximized.

The idea that "customers are buying outcomes, not software," compelled Motive to set up its industry's first customer care unit. Working from the success metrics that are specified during Motive's sales process, customer care employees are charged with ensuring that customers attain the returns that they anticipated when they purchased Motive solutions. Maples says:

The Customer Care folks come in and agree on a set of metrics with the customer before we deploy the software. Then, on an ongoing basis, they come back in quarterly business reviews. They'll say, "We are three months after going live, and we expect the following business outcomes. Where are we above plan, and where are we below plan?"

They come out with a set of improvement programs. We have done this with over 100 customers, so we have a whole lot of information about what it costs to run a program, how many people will respond, etc. We can help the customer think through the tradeoffs. We want to make sure they understand they have the choice to vary the mix of programs and activities and to modify business outcome forecasts accordingly.

THE FINAL GOAL
Prime Solution Renewal

The process of value enhancement is synonymous with the creation of new and improved solutions. Further, the best opportunities for solution renewal are usually discovered within the customer's business. The final phase of the Prime Solution Cycle is a rich hunting ground for these opportunities.

Commonly encountered implementation difficulties can be treated as renewal opportunities in disguise. The success of call center CRM solutions, for example, depends heavily on employee adoption and use. When direct retailer Lands' End purchased Trilogy Software's CRM solution for its customer support center, it also hired Deloitte Consulting to create a series of "Day in the Life of . . ." visioning exercises to teach employees how the software could enhance their interactions with customers. Trilogy, in turn, built the value of the training into their solution by integrating suggestions from the Deloitte exercises into the first release of the software itself.[11]

Customer demands for results metrics and ROI enhancements are also opportunities for solution renewal. International Truck and Engine Corporation, for example, is turning its customers' desires for real-time results into the first comprehensive telematics solution available from an OEM in its industry. The system, developed in collaboration with IBM, is powered by a black box within a truck that gathers a wide variety of data such as vehicle position, performance metrics, and maintenance diagnostics. Wireless transmissions of the collected data are received at International's Web portal, where the information is delivered into a dedicated customer portfolio. Fleet managers can access the site to check vehicle location, ensure driver and vehicle security, and diagnose breakdowns. The collected data also facilitates the analysis and reduction of downtime and operating costs and the tracking and improvement of other productivity and performance measures.[12]

Service/support and sales, the two functions that play the primary roles in the final phases of the Prime Solution Cycle, are closest to customers and, as a result, tend to be the first to discover solution opportunities. Unfortunately, many companies don't have the culture or the systems in place to collect these observations. They often ignore, and sometimes actively discourage, the transmission of these opportunities. All too often, the pressure on sales and support teams to find the next prospect and close the next big sale precludes any quality involvement and in-depth observations with current customers.

To capitalize on these valuable sources of opportunity information, companies need to create conduits for the transmission and consideration of field data. These feedback mechanisms represent the final link in the Prime Solution Cycle. They connect the end of the value chain back to its beginning by creating an information flow that ensures that new solution opportunities are transmitted back into the Prime Solution Cycle. This information serves as the basis for the development of new Prime Solutions. Thus, the conclusion of one revolution around the Prime Solution Cycle becomes the impetus for another.

A Prime Solution represents a quantum leap forward for most providers of complex products and services. It provides the means to break down the functional silos in both your organization and the customer's.

Think of how you would respond to a solution provider who brought these capabilities to your door. A resource with these capabilities could undoubtedly make a major impact on your business performance and your personal success. They would not only ensure that you selected the best solution for your hard-earned dollars, but they would also assist in achieving a successful implementation, help you quantify and maximize your return on investment, and finally, ensure the sustainability of your optimized performance. This resource sounds like a highly valued business partner, a source of continual competitive advantage. Isn't this the position we all want to occupy in our customers' minds?

In today's intensely competitive world, we might be tempted to think that creating and delivering Prime Solutions is a desirable but unattainable ideal. I trust the definitions we've provided, the suggestions we've made, and the examples we've cited all speak to the achievable reality of a Prime Solution strategy.

I believe it is appropriate to close this book with the same key thought I used to close *Mastering the Complex Sale: There Is No Magic:*

Spectacular success is always preceded by unspectacular preparation.

So enjoy your preparation—and enjoy your success!

N o t e s

Preface

1. Chandru Krishnamurthy, Juliet Johansson, and Hank Schlissberg, "Solutions Selling: Is the Pain Worth the Gain?" *McKinsey Quarterly* (http://www.mckinsey.com/practices/mar keting/ourknowledge/pdf/Solutions_SolutionsSelling.pdf), April 2003.

Chapter I

1. Peter F. Drucker, *Management: Tasks, Responsibilities, Practices* (New York: Harper & Row, 1974), 83–84.

2. Thomas J. Watson, Jr., *A Business and Its Beliefs* (New York: McGraw-Hill, 1963), 68.

3. Louis V. Gerstner, Jr., *Who Says Elephants Can't Dance? Inside IBM's Historic Turnaround* (New York: Harper Business, 2002), 258.

4. Ibid., 132.

5. Lisa Picarille, "The Goldilocks Syndrome." *Customer Relationship Management,* January 2004, 29–31.

6. Michael G. Wells, "Business Process Reengineering Implementations Using Internet Technology," *Business Process Management Journal* 6, no. 2 (2000): 164.

7. Craig Stedman, "Failed ERP Gamble Haunts Hershey," *ComputerWorld.com,* 1 November 1999.

8. Marc L. Songini, "Nike Says Profit Woes IT-Based," *ComputerWorld.com,* 5 March 2001.

9. David Cay Johnston, "At IRS, a Systems Update Gone Awry," *New York Times,* 11 December 2003.

10. John P. Kotter, *Leading Change* (Boston, 1996, Harvard Business Press), 4.

11. Donna Greiner and Theodore Kinni, *1,001 Ways to Keep Customers Coming Back* (Roseville: Prima Publishing, 1999), 89.

12. Steve Konicki, "Nike Just Didn't Do It Right, Says i2 Technologies." *InformationWeek.com,* 5 March 2001.

13. Craig Stedman, "ERP Flops Point to Users' Plans." *ComputerWorld.com,* 15 November 1999.

Chapter 2

1. Peter F. Drucker, *The Practice of Management* (New York: Harper & Row, 1954); Clayton Christensen, *The Innovator's Dilemma* (Boston: Harvard Business School Publishing, 1997).

2. The word processing progression first appeared in the author's interview for *SoftwareMarketSolution.com* (www.prime resource.com/software-market-solution-part-1.htm).

3. Peter F. Drucker, *Management: Tasks, Responsibilities, Practices* (New York: Harper & Row, 1974), 64–65.

4. John Sullivan, foreword to *Mastering the Complex Sale,* by John Thull (Hoboken, New Jersey: John Wiley & Sons, 2003), vi–ix.

5. Theodore Levitt, *The Marketing Imagination: New, Expanded Edition* (New York: Free Press, 1986), 78–85.

6. Theodore Levitt, "Marketing Myopia," *Harvard Business Review,* September-October 1975, 14.

7. Clayton M. Christensen, *The Innovator's Dilemma* (Boston: Harvard Business School Press, 1997), xxiii.

8. Jeff Thull, "Complex Strategies for High Stakes Sales," a Microsoft Office Live Meeting Webinar held on 28 October

2003. A link to the audio transcript is available at www.prime
resource.com/prime-resource-library.htm.

9. Levitt, *The Marketing Imagination,* 115.

10. "Dell Wants Growth," *InformationWeek,* 12 January 2004,
10.

Chapter 3

1. Donna Greiner and Theodore Kinni, *Ayn Rand and Business* (New York: Texere, 2001), 62–63.

2. Jon Derome, "Speeds, Feeds, and Technology Prowess
Fail to Impress ERP Buyers," The Yankee Group research note,
15 January 2004; "ERP Brands Have Weak Customer Affilia-
tion, Say The Yankee Group," The Yankee Group press release,
15 January 2004.

3. Matt Hamblen, "Sales Automation Projects Still Struggle," *ComputerWorld,* 2 November 1998.

4. Sean T. Kelly and John A. Barry, "Failing to Construct
the Seller," *ComputerWorld,* 12 March 2001.

5. Jeff Thull, *Mastering the Complex Sale.* See pages 25–31
for a detailed exploration of customer comprehension and the
Decision Challenge.

6. Mila D'Antonio, "Price, Complexity, Wal-Mart Dictate
RFID Adoption," *Inside 1to1,* 17 January 2004.

7. Robert Dolan and Hermann Simon, *Power Pricing* (New
York: Free Press, 1996), 37.

Chapter 4

1. "Cornerstones of Postsales Service Excellence," UPS
Supply Chain Solutions white paper, 2003 (http://www.ups-
scs.com/solutions/white_papers/wp_cornerstone_postsales
.pdf), 5.

2. Chuck Salter, "Surprise Package," *Fast Company,* February 2004, 62.

3. Steve Kemper, *Code Name Ginger* (Boston: Harvard Business School Press, 2003), 5–6.

4. Ibid., 305.

5. Theodore Kinni, "Setting the Right Price at the Right Time," *Harvard Management Update,* December 2003, 5.

6. This number is based on the number of Segways involved in a 2003 recall of all models to fix a glitch in its operation.

7. "UPS Logistics Chooses Parts-Planning Platform," *InternetWeek.com,* 16 April 2002.

8. The Georgia-Pacific Resins, Inc. example is based on Prime Resource Group's work with the company.

Chapter 5

1. Herbert W. Lovelace, "Trapped in the Sales Presentation from Hell," *InformationWeek,* 10 November 2003, 122.

2. The Graham Company example is drawn from Prime Resource Group's interviews and case studies.

3. Michael Schrage, "Daniel Kahneman: The Thought Leader Interview," *Strategy + Business* (http://www.strategy-business.com/press/article/03409?pg=0), Winter 2003, 6.

4. Dan Lovallo and Daniel Kahneman, "Delusions of Success," *Harvard Business Review,* July 2003, 56–63.

5. The Shell Global Solutions example is drawn from interviews by Jeff Thull, June 2004.

Chapter 6

1. Steve Marlin, "Mission: Transformation," *InformationWeek,* 2 February 2004, 31–32.

2. Martin Garvey, "EMC's Metamorphosis," *Information-Week*, 2 February 2004, 38.

3. "Unlocking the ePC RFID Opportunity Requires Migration Management," Yankee Group report, February 2004.

4. "New fuel helps Schumacher win the Formula One World Championship" http://www.shellglobalsolutions.com/news_room/news_stories/2003_1/ferrari148.htm.

5. "The History of Jim Waters and Waters Corporation: 1958–2003," http://www.waters.com/WatersDivision/ContentD.asp?ref=KHAS-5R2PA2.

6. The Waters example is based on author interviews and Prime Resource Group case file.

7. Robert D. Austin and Richard L. Nolan, "Manage ERP Initiatives as New Ventures, Not IT Projects," HBS Working Paper, 17 December 1998.

8. Ibid., 3.

9. Bruce Hudson, "Finding ROI in RFIS Is Harder Than . . ." *METAbits*, 3 February 2004.

10. Paul McDougall, "RFID Services from Afar," *InformationWeek*, 12 January 2004, 45.

11. Darrell Dunn, "In Search of Flexibility," *Information-Week*, 2 February 2004, 12.

12. "News in Brief," *Customer Relationship Management*, February 2004, 17.

13. Tony Kontzer, "Collaboration System Cuts Unexpected Costs," *InformationWeek*, 5 January 2004, 28.

14. "Relationship Capital Management," Aberdeen Group Executive white paper, January 2004, 9.

15. "Staples Fastens on Fujitsu to Expand IT Services Partnership," *Business Wire*, 16 December 2003; "Staples and Fujitsu Collaborate to Reduce IT Service Costs," Fujitsu Transaction Solutions case study, March 2003; Judith Mottl, "IT Outsourc-

ing Gives Staples the Tools to Grow," *InformationWeek*, 15 May 2000.

16. The Datascope example is based on Prime Resource Group engagement with the company and the corporate Web site (www.datascope.com). Also, Jayne Prendergast, "Benchmark Update," *Counterpulsation Outcomes Registry News*, July 2000, 1–4.

17. Robert White and Barry James, "The Outsourcing Manual," Hampshire, England, 1996 Gower House.

Chapter 7

1. Clayton M. Christensen and Michael Raynor, *The Innovator's Dilemma* (Boston: Harvard Business School Press, 2003), 73.

2. Rick Whiting, "IBM Debuts More Middleware Packages for Vertical Industries," *InformationWeek*, 1 March 2004.

3. Steve Lohr, "Big Blue's Big Bet," *New York Times*, 25 January 2004.

4. "PARC History" at www.parc.xerox.com. Also, Douglas K. Smith and Robert C. Alexander, *Fumbling the Future* (New York: William Morrow, 1988); Michael A. Hiltzik, *Dealers in Lightning* (New York: Harper Business, 2000).

5. Kevin Maney, "Homebred CEO Summons IBM's Past, Present, Future," *USA Today*, 19 November 2003.

6. Joan Clark, Baptist Hospital vice president for patient care and chief nursing officer, interview by Jeff Thull, August 2003; Ted Kinni, "Bedside Manner Goes High Tech," *Inside 1to1*, 6 October 2003.

7. Lohr, "Big Blue's Big Bet," *New York Times*.

8. Beth Bachelor, "Boeing's Flight Plan," *InformationWeek*, 20 February 2004, 20–21; The Boeing Company's corporate Web site (www.boeing.com).

9. Carleen Hawn, "If He's So Smart . . . Steve Jobs, Apple, and the Limits of Innovation," *Fast Company,* January 2004, 68.

10. Chris Zook, *Beyond the Core* (Boston: Harvard Business School Press, 2004), 54–56. Also, The Hilti Group corporate Web site (www.hilti.com).

11. Leslie Nichols, "Boeing Redefines 'The Box' with Its New 7E7 Dreamliner Airplane," Boeing Company press release, July 2003.

12. "Business Value of Customer Benefits," Knowledge@ Wharton and Microsoft Collaboration (http://knowledge.whar ton.upenn.edu/microsoft/070302.html), 3 July 2002.

Chapter 8

1. Theodore Levitt, *The Marketing Imagination: New, Expanded Edition* (New York: Free Press, 1986), 128.

2. Adrian J. Slywotzky, *Value Migration* (Boston: Harvard Business School Press, 1996), 3–4.

3. For greater detail on the Progression to Change, see Jeff Thull, *Mastering the Complex Sale,* 46–49.

4. The Microsoft Press example is drawn from a Prime Resource Group engagement with that business unit.

5. Theodore Kinni, "How Strategic Is Your Sales Strategy" Harvard Management Update, February 2004; Ernest Waaser, Michael Pekkarinen, and Michael Weissel, "A Smarter Way to Sell," Mercer Management Consulting, article manuscript, January 2004.

6. Clayton M. Christensen, *The Innovator's Solution* (Boston: Harvard Business School Press, 2003), 75.

7. Sources for the Angiomax example include Adam Feurstein, "The Medicines Company Pushes Its Blood-Thinner," *The Street.com,* 12 November 2002; John T. Gourville, *The Medicines Company,* Harvard Business School case study 9-502-006; The-

odore Kinni, "Setting the Right Price at the Right Time," *Harvard Management Update,* December 2003.

8. "Bottom-Line Marketing Drives Better B-to-B Selling," Aberdeen Group Executive white paper, November 2003, 3.

9. The Cisco example is drawn from Tony Szekalski and Joshua Rossman, "CMM and Value Selling Help Cisco Switch Gears," a CMM Forum presentation (www.cmmforum.net), August 2003.

Chapter 9

1. *The Customer-Selected World-Class Sales Excellence Ten-Year Research Report* (Dayton, Ohio: HR Chally Group, 2002).

2. For additional information on the "go for the no" concept, its ramifications, and utilization, see Jeff Thull, "How to Prevent Unpaid Consulting," http://www.primeresource.com.

3. Jeff Thull's *Mastering the Complex Sale* is dedicated to an in-depth description of Diagnostic Business Development and the role of the sales function in Prime Solutions.

4. "Trinidad's Petrotrin aims for higher profits" http://www .shellglobalsolutions.com/news_room/news_stories/2003_2/ petrotrin163.htm; also, "Petrotrin embarks on five-year refinery plan" *Impact,* Issue 2, 2004.

5. Author interview with Kevin McPoyle, November 2002; Prime Resource Group's *Best Practices Report.*

6. Darrell Dunn, "What's Next in CRM?" *InformationWeek,* 3 November 2003, 47.

7. Author interview with Kevin McPoyle, November 2002; Prime Resource Group's *Best Practices Report.*

8. Prime Resource Group customer interview, September 2003.

Chapter 10

1. Michael A. Cusumano, *The Business of Software* (New York: Free Press, 2004), 82.

2. "The Real ROI from i2 Supply Chain Management," Nucleus Research, Research Note D1, October 2002.

3. Cusumano, *The Business of Software,* 19–21.

4. Jon Derome, "Speeds, Feeds, and Technology Prowess Fail to Impress ERP Buyers," The Yankee Group research note, 15 January 2004.

5. The Project Management Institute (www.pmi.org) is an excellent source for change methodologies and best practices.

6. John F. Kotter, *Leading Change* (Harvard Business Press, 1996), 20–21.

7. Sumantra Sengupta, "To Err Is Human . . . ," *Optimize,* January 2004.

8. Ibid.

9. Paul McDougall, "Optimizing through Outsourcing," *InformationWeek,* 1 March 2004, 53–56; "EDS Announces $320 Million, Multiyear Contract with Blue Cross Blue Shield of Massachusetts," press release, 18 December 2003.

10. The Motive, Inc. example is drawn from The Prime Resource Group's engagement with the company and author interviews.

11. David Myron, "Vertical Focus: Integrators: Necessary Evil or Indispensable Resources?" *DestinationCRM.com,* 1 March 2004.

12. "International Telematics Puts Fleet Managers inside Every Truck," International Truck and Engine Corp. press release, 14 March 2004; Linda Rosencrance, "International Truck to Offer Full Range of Telematics," *ComputerWorld,* 15 March 2004.